Crafting by the Moon

Heather Moon

Published in 2021 by FeedARead.com Publishing

A CIP catalogue record for this title is available from the British Library.

Contents

Introduction

"Oh no, not another book about moon magic, astrology and the Wheel of the Year….." I hear you cry! This isn't a book about those things, yet it is - in a different guise. I hope you find my little beginner's book practical, teaching you how to learn to live in natural rhythm with the energies of the universe so that your intuitive spiritual energy is enhanced.

Let me explain. I've followed this spiritual path for as long as I can remember. When I was younger, I didn't really have a name for it, it was something just so completely natural to me and felt "right". I can't identify when this path unravelled before me, it was just there and was the perfect way for me to live.

And so over the years I've learnt bits here and there - from people I met, from reading books and magazines, from visiting mystical shops, from courses and workshops, from friends with an esoteric interest, from spiritualist churches I've attended from time to time, from simply trying things out, sometimes with success, sometimes not, from working in a group and working as a solitary and of course in more recent years, from researching the internet - but I've never found one book that pulled together all the basic aspects of the spiritual path I'd found myself walking for many years.

I'd found books and articles on moon magic; in other places I found more detailed information about working with the moon phases; then elsewhere I found information about the importance of the astrological sign the moon was in and the void of course moon; from a group I joined I learnt about the Wheel of the Year….and then I found out bits and pieces on intention and spell casting and the tools of the trade. And so I found out a bit here, a bit there - I cut out any relevant articles, information and spells and I crafted my own series of books, being wonderful reference documents for myself. However, it still felt uncoordinated! So I continued to learn and practice - this had become so much a part of me and my lifestyle.

My fundamental interest in spirituality has been with me throughout my life and remained a constant during the ebbs and flows of that life. At times, much more time could be invested in my passion; at other times due to all the demands of my personal life and the general pace of life, my spiritual activities were very much as and when I had time.

Life changed dramatically for me in the mid-1990s. After a lot of grief and soul searching, I finally found the courage to leave an abusive marriage. So, with two children to look after, a mortgage to pay, a house to run on my own, a new career path, plus five cats to contend with, the road opened up and gave me more opportunity to learn, grow, expand and practice the magical knowledge I had accumulated through all the ups and downs of my life. It was to be a wonderful adventure.

The years rolled on. My children left home and set up their own. I married again - to the most kind, thoughtful man who has been hugely tolerant of my spiritual beliefs and supported me throughout. We moved home, my grandchildren arrived and I finally decided to volunteer for redundancy and early retirement after 20 years in my then professional role. I had completely fallen out of love with the corporate world. It was time for a change.

During the time I was reaching my decision to leave the corporate world, which took place over several years, I found myself training to be a Reiki Master Teacher, to teach meditation, how to give a crystal therapy treatment and how to give an Indian head massage. I'd never set out to do this – indeed, I resisted Reiki for many years – but somehow I just found myself on these courses with no idea where I was heading, but all of this simply evolved as my life in the corporate world dissolved.

With my career experience in training, plus writing and delivering training packages and my innate interest in spirituality, the next step seemed to be to set up my own small business. I didn't know if it was right or wrong, but I simply trusted this was the right way. I remember someone I really respected saying to me "don't think about it, just do it". That was the spur I needed. I didn't want it to swamp my life, but I could see no point in having all the spiritual knowledge and experience I'd gained to simply not share it with others. What would be the point of taking all this with me to the grave? It had to be shared.

I was very conscious that there was a rising interest in the spiritual path I'd been following for most of my life and I sensed a thirst for this knowledge from the people I'd met over more recent years. There was a lot of interest and support for my intention and so I spent several months setting up my little business – MoonCrafting. What an experience it was to be. I'd never been self-employed before, knew nothing about public liability insurance, how to set up and furnish a therapy room, how to do my accounts, design a website, business cards and flyers, advertise and promote myself (so completely alien to me more than anything else) and write my own training programmes and manuals. Eventually I launched my new venture and have enjoyed every moment of it since – www.mooncrafting.com.

As my business settled and became steady, I still had a restlessness within me and as I was running both my meditation, tarot and spiritual development teaching sessions, it became clearer what this was about - a seed was being planted. I'd been an avid reader all my life – whether that was books, magazines, internet articles – I'd always had a thirst to know more. I was also aware that one of my strengths was my written communication from life-long feedback.

So how about combining these areas? I started to spend time meditating and contemplating what was to be my next step. Feedback from my teaching sessions was positive, which re-enforced my belief in what I should be doing……and then one day I clearly received an intuitive message to write a book incorporating everything I'd been teaching - and so here it is!

I've written my book for the ordinary man and woman who've become frustrated by the focus on materialism and want to find a more peaceful, spiritual way to live. So this is a beginner's guide to help you progress on this path if that's what you choose to do. This journey is a way of life, with its purpose to reach a place of unconditional love - to really believe our world and all other beings are sacred. We're all here to use our intuition, to link to spirit, the goddess, the universe, "those upstairs", the higher dimensions, your higher self, the management – whatever you choose to call "it".

Don't be under the impression that living this life is easy. It won't be, but I can assure you it's very fulfilling to connect with our universe and everything within it. So take from this book what resonates with you – there's no set doctrine on this pathway.

I hope you enjoy your journey, one that has completely fulfilled me - of learning to live in tune with the natural rhythm of the universal energies, in tune with your own energy as well as that of the moon, the sun, the "divine", with nature and our Mother Earth, being the one who sustains us all....and as time rolls by and you become accustomed to the teachings in this book working in your life, you'll find your knowledge and experience increasing and expanding over time as I have.

Simply enjoy!!

Chapter 1 - Energetic You!

In order to fully understand where you fit in the context of this book and our wonderful universe, you need to have some basic background knowledge about energy, our aura, auric fields and chakras to understand the link between these and the lunar, solar and earth energies. I'll try to keep it as simple as possible – so, let's start our journey at the beginning with you and your energy.

In simplest terms, energy travels to earth as pure white sunlight, which contains electromagnetic energy. It travels down in different wavelengths, some being visible and others invisible. As humans, we can only see about 40% of the electromagnetic spectrum.

Everything on Mother Earth has its own vibration – life is a vibration. Matter is not static – it's a mass of moving particles, atoms and molecules that all emit their own light, heat and colours. These vibrations constantly interact with each other and connect. When we become aware of this energy, we can learn to protect ourselves from bad vibrations and attract good ones.

So when white light energy flows through us, connecting us with universal energy, I believe we can be healthier. This energy is recognised by many therapeutic systems and spiritual ways of life (Reiki, crystal therapy, reflexology). A state of disharmony and being unbalanced occurs when our energy becomes blocked.

Learning about energy is fun. We can explore spiritual realms and expand our consciousness, which is what you can do when you've read this book and start putting it into practice.

We all learn in different ways - some of us by doing, others by reading, some by listening. This is sometimes a difficult concept when what you're learning about is invisible and inaudible. You and everything about you – your body, your thoughts and emotions

– are a product of energy moving between the known and unknown. For instance, you can't see air, but you know it's there because you're breathing (just a simple way of explaining the presence of energy in our lives).

We are surrounded by what is called an aura. An aura is the human energy field which surrounds our entire body. It's a two way transmitter and receiver connecting us to all the vibrations around us.

We know it exists, but what is it? For well over 100 years scientists have been substantiating its existence and consider it to be a bio-magnetic field surrounding the human body which extends indefinitely.

They've also decided it conveys information about what's taking place inside your body, rather than outside, so the purpose of the aura is linked to your internal health and it contains information from each organ, gland and tissue in your body.

There are three major planes in the aura, extending out from the body, and these relate to your physical, emotional and mental health. There's no clear definition of them as they blend into one another but they're the physical, astral and spiritual planes.

In addition, there are also seven bands of energy known as the auric bodies, layers or fields that make up these three major planes and all these extend out from the body. Each auric field links to one of the seven internal chakras. The naval chakra is a relatively new chakra that you don't need to worry about at the moment and is the eighth internal chakra.

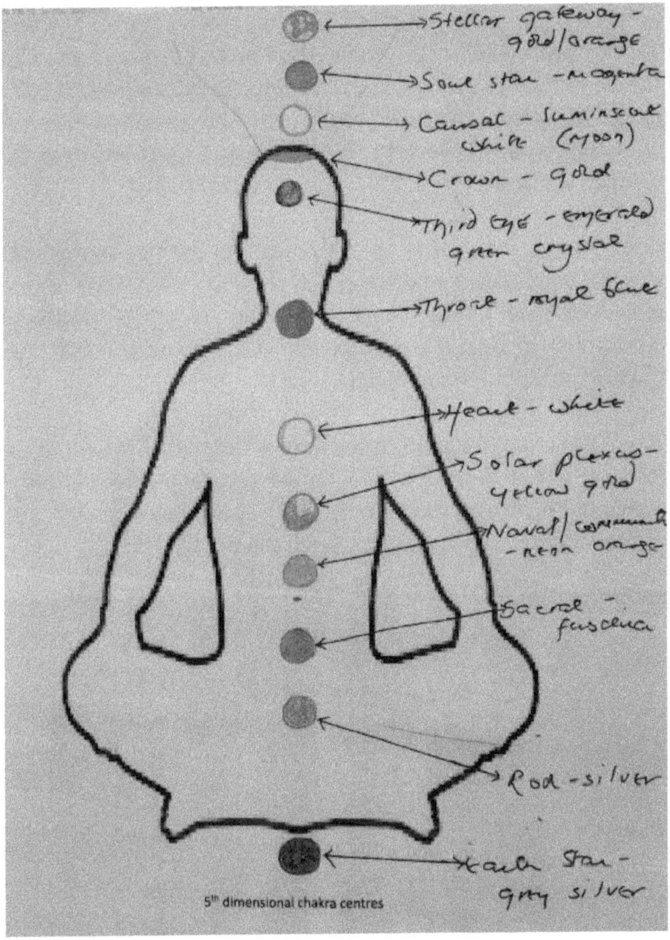

5th dimensional chakra centres

The auric field closest to your physical body is known as the etheric field and it's an exact replica of your physical body, except we can't see it. It can't distinguish between good and bad vibrations and it acts as a collector and transmitter of energy from the other "bodies" in the aura. It's at this level practitioners work so they can cleanse and balance the energy before it's transmitted into your physical body.

We all have eleven main energy bodies in our auras known as chakras (although you will find different numbers quoted if you do further research). The seven main internal chakras (excluding the naval chakra) are believed to govern bodily functions near their region in the spine.

Unfortunately many of us are only aware of our five senses but in order to be in balance between our physical, mental and spiritual bodies, we need to keep our energy body – or aura - healthy too. The external chakras are spiritual and at this point, you don't need to worry about them too much.

One of the main functions of the aura is to collect light energy and send it to the chakras. The chakras are constantly moving and are vital to our health and well-being. Each chakra is associated with a different colour and glands/organs in the physical body.

An energy exercise for you to try

To experience energy, you might like to try out this fun exercise and see what you can feel.

Rub your hands together vigorously for about a minute. Then, with your palms facing each other, hold your hands out in front of you, shoulder width apart. Slowly bring your hands together until you can "feel" something with your hands – possibly your hands may feel as though they are resting on something or you may feel some resistance or tension when bringing your hands together. That's energy you're sensing.

And so that's all about you and your energy. There's clearly much more to your energy – and many more chakras - if you want to study it further. However, for the purpose of this book, you've enough understanding to continue. Let's move on to learn about how your energy can positively blend with other energies around us.

Chapter 2 - A Bit About Our Lady Moon

We all experience the power of the moon in our daily lives – its gravitational pull influences the tides, so why shouldn't it influence us when our make-up is around 60% water? Why shouldn't the moon have an impact on our emotional and spiritual wellbeing? She's our nearest planet, purely being a reflection of sunlight. Her magnetic and spiritual powers are always affecting us, even if we don't acknowledge it. Our moon is as well known to us as the road on which we live, but few of us recognise her impact on our lives although there is a rise in numbers over recent years.

Research has proved some facts about the impact the moon has on our lives. It's shown that we eat more food and drink far less alcohol at full moon. Medically, asthma attacks increase during the new and full moons, GP consultations increase around a full moon alongside increases in both crime and hospital admissions – probably a pretty ghastly time to be on duty.

Traditionally mental health issues were associated with the full moon which appears to worsen any symptoms - hence the old reference to "luna"tics – with Luna being one of the moon goddesses.

Research has also shown that sleep drops by approximately 30% around the time of the full moon. We're more generous and patient and have more energy than at any other time in the lunar cycle. Surgery at the time of the waning crescent moon is less traumatic with less blood loss and you also have the new moon around the corner to help with its healing. I'll go through the moon phases thoroughly in Chapter 3.

The moon also has an impact on the female body. The average length of the menstrual cycle is 28 days, mirroring the average length of one new moon cycle to the next. In some cultures in the world, the menstrual cycle is referred to as "moon time". Sadly though, the contraceptive pill, artificial lighting and air travel – to name a few - have thrown our natural cycles completely out of balance. We have many women with irregular cycles, womb related issues and fertility problems. Working with the sensitivities of these feminine issues is certainly a growth area in the health and wellness sector.

Although the reasons for all these effects aren't clear, scientists do think it's related to the gravitational pull of the moon having an effect on our hormones and immune system. So consequently, put simply, there's a tide within each of us that ebbs and flows and we need to learn how to live with that tide.

The moon represents all that is feminine just as the sun represents all that is masculine. The moon is ever changing. It embodies our emotions, is mystical, mysterious and secretive representing darkness, receptiveness and intuition. All these might be words used to describe the feminine energy. The sun's energy is completely different – it's vibrant, passionate, enthusiastic, risk taking, active, solid, unchanging and masculine. We need a balance of these energies in our lives.

If you've too much female energy, you can appear passive, not speaking up when you need to, being easily afraid and offended by what others say about you. You may be overly submissive, being easily hurt and over-sensitive. You might put everyone else before yourself – this is the "mother" nature – and caring for others without receiving that care back.

If you've too much male energy, you may be aggressive, too assertive and seem harsh, critical and out of touch with your emotions. It's a dominant, task focused energy and when it's out of balance can lead to you feeling shut down or "blocked".

In ancient times we lived our lives by the lunar calendar – it helped us know when to go hunting, when to plant crops, when to pick those crops. Sadly over time and with the arrival of technology which is so intrinsic in all our lives, we've lost a great deal of our ancestral knowledge. Now it's time to reclaim that knowledge as many of us are.

The moon has always been the focus of worship for many ancient civilisations. They paid tribute to her as a major goddess, often representing women in their various phases of life – from maiden (or daughter) to mother to crone (grandmother). She is known as the triple goddess and you may recognise her symbol.

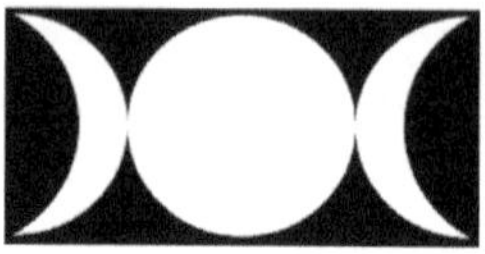

To explain what this means a little more, the maiden aspect of our lives is represented by the waxing crescent moon. The maiden phase is all about new beginnings, inspiration, being young, innovation, pleasure and purity. She encourages you to explore your creativity and desires – and starts to lead you to discover your spirituality. The mother phase is represented by the full moon. This phase embodies fertility, nurturing, healing, self-care, love, protection and responsibility. It is in this phase we learn to be self-disciplined and patient and the mother phase wants you to experience the giving and receiving of love. The final phase is the crone phase represented by the waning crescent moon. It's the time of fulfilment, wisdom, knowledge, recognising the truth, death and endings – the time to accept that without death, there is no re-birth.

Lunar energy is still important in a great deal of spiritual practice – Buddhist festivals are held on the full moon; in Christianity, Easter is set after the first full moon that takes place after the Spring Equinox - and in Wicca the moon is the focal point.

We're going to look at these old ways which will allow you to start planning your actions around the lunar cycle and seeing how you can achieve positive results in your life. I would suggest that you buy yourself a journal. Record through the month how you feel and watch the phases of the moon and their astrological sign (more in Chapter 3). This will help you work with the lunar phases and integrate them into your daily life. If you follow this, you'll begin to see why some things have gone well and why others haven't been as productive. You'll see how doing something under the wrong phase of the moon or when the moon is in an astrological sign that isn't conducive to what you're trying to achieve, doesn't produce the result you were expecting.

I would also recommend investing in a moon diary – one that gives you the phases and signs of the moon in your time zone. For some time I followed the moon phases and astrological signs and then realised I was working from American time zones – not very helpful for my practice in the UK!

In addition, I have a moon deck – a lovely deck of cards that I use every day. The cards help you plot the phase of the moon, the meaning of the phase and the astrological sign of the moon. However, you do need to be disciplined about using them and make it a daily habit so you can learn and intuitively know the next moon phase and the sign it'll be in. It soon becomes second nature and is now so usual to me, it's like putting the kettle on in the morning for a cup of coffee.

Moon (or lunar) energy - to me - is the fastest paced energy. The moon moves through each astrological sign approximately every 2.5 days through its 28/29 day cycle as well as moving through the different phases in its cycle at the same time. The sun's energy is a slower paced energy, moving through all 12 astrological signs over the course of a year and earth energy is the slowest energy, working through 8 main festivals in a year. Your own energy needs to work with these energies and walk within their energy cycles. Once you can master this, everything else falls naturally into place.

Chapter 3 - The Moon Phases through the Lunar Cycle

Now for a more in depth look at the phases of the moon. This used to confuse me in the past at times - there are different opinions on how many moon phases there actually are. I'd become confused about the dark of the moon, the dark moon and new moon, couldn't remember the difference between waxing and waning and so on – then one day it just all fell into place, so I hope my understanding will help you so you don't have the complexities I had to unravel in order to get to grips with the lunar cycle.

<u>The Lunar Cycle</u> – this is the cycle of phases the moon moves through, starting at the new or dark moon, the moon starts to wax, which means it grows bigger until it reaches full moon. It then begins to reduce in size, so this is the waning cycle until it disappears from view and a new lunar cycle begins. So, the waxing moon phase is the time when she is growing and expanding to become full and her power grows accordingly. The waning moon phase is when the full moon has passed and she's now diminishing with the same happening to her power - and we return to the dark of the moon and move towards the start of the next lunar cycle.

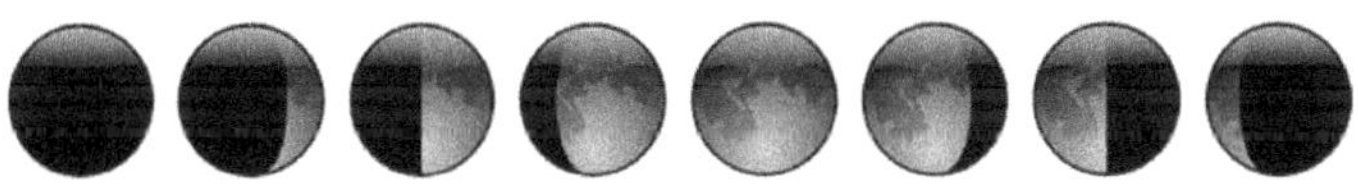

<u>The New Moon</u> – At the time of the new moon, you can see nothing. The moon appears invisible. This is also the time known as the <u>dark moon</u>. The moon is hidden by the brilliance of the sun for a few hours, but then as it draws away from the sun's light, its silver crescent can just be seen.

It's a time when ideas are born, seeds are sown, intentions are made (more about intention setting in Chapter 7). The new moon occurs a couple of days before it first appears as a crescent and is when the sky is at its darkest. It's a time of introversion and sensitivity, a time for reflection, meditation and to make plans for the coming lunar cycle.

Use this fresh lunar energy to ask for things to be brought into your life. It's the time for new beginnings, for seed sowing. You might want to set something in motion such as a new business venture, a new job, a new relationship or a new home. It's the best time for decisions to be made and any planning to start. Be open to new ideas, spending time preparing mentally and spiritually for what you want to manifest in your life. For instance, if you want to lose some weight, now would be the best time to start a healthy eating plan. You could also use this moon phase to re-start a project which may have been put to one side.

In terms of how you may be feeling around the time of the new moon, it may be that you're a bit low because of the lack of lunar light – just like some of us feel when we move into the dark, colder months of the year and we just want to retreat into our "cave", re-emerging in the spring. It's a time when you're likely to argue with those you love and develop some negative thoughts. You might also find you've more difficulty getting up in the morning and feel depleted emotionally and physically. However, this is the ideal time to focus on your psychic development if that's what you wish to do. So have some quality "me time" and pamper yourself in whatever way feels right for you. Any pampering is sure to raise your energy levels.

Take time to meditate on your dreams and tune in to your higher self (or whatever/whomever you believe in) so you can ask for - and receive - some guidance about moving forward with your plans.

Write your wish/dream down - or you might prefer to draw it. Really feel it has come to fruition and see it clearly in your mind's eye. Read what you're wishing/dreaming for out loud as this is very powerful. Words have power. Now's the time to think about your wishes/dreams and the potential for them to manifest and become reality.

And so, on the night of the new moon, you may like to cleanse yourself and the space where you'll be working (I give examples about how you can do this in Chapter 12) to send your wishes to the universe. Make your wishes just after the time of the new moon (up to 8 hours preferably but can be up to 48 hours). Write your wishes down so your personal energy is attached to them. Or if you prefer, draw a picture that represents your wish.

Up to the time of the full moon, keep coming back to your wish and re-affirming it. Be very clear what it is you want. Don't make wishes about other people's behaviour. The Wiccan Rede says "An it harm none, do what ye will" which I believe is a very good way to live your life. Instead you may want to look at your own behaviour as there may be something you could change that has an impact on others around you. So be clear in your wishes – always write in the present tense. Once your intention is written, if the words don't sound right, then change them. It's very important you're happy with what you've written or drawn.

You should also expect that some wishes/dreams may take some time to manifest. During this time you'll learn to be patient, which is always a good life lesson, and if your wish doesn't materialise at all, it may be that it wasn't for your highest good. I've had wishes that haven't come true and despite feeling a bit down about it for a while, I've learnt over the years that there are reasons for an unfulfilled wish and I'm far more gracious about my expectations these days. Often it's not until some time has passed that you realise what those reasons were. You, too, will learn the same lesson over time if you continue to walk this path.

The Waxing Crescent Moon – This is the time when the crescent moon is growing. It's that sliver of a crescent emerging from the darkness a couple of days after the new moon. Now is the time to overcome any challenges or resolve any issues you may be having since setting your intention. It's also a good time to give your wish a bit of an "energy boost" as the moon continues to wax to her full phase. Make affirmations about your new project. Set your dreams/wishes in motion.

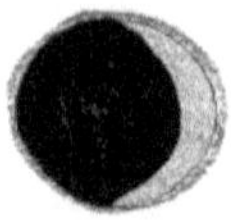

Have the courage to move forward with your dreams and really believe they will manifest in your life. The moon is moving from having been invisible to her full power and it's the same for your wishes and dreams. Keep thinking about what you want. Go back to the wish list you made at the new moon and re-visit it. Read it out aloud again and visualise your wishes/dreams coming true. If you want to transform your life, you need to see it happening and consolidate your intention. Visualise it as if you're living it and feel all the feelings you'd feel when it's manifested. If you want something you have to really go for it - so hold on and don't give up. Be determined to succeed.

The First Quarter Moon - This phase is when the moon looks like half a football in the sky and is slowly growing to be full. It's also sometimes known as the waxing half moon. It's quite usual around this moon phase to doubt your dreams and not feel as determined or passionate about it as you did when you set your intention. If you're still going after your dream, you really need to commit to it. Refer back to your wish list - re-read it and really feel your intentions, re-visualise them, re-state them out loud..... see them being your reality.

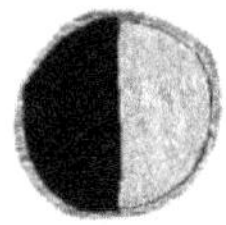

Any issues that come up now will need some action taken as this moon is about development. The astrological reason for this is that the moon is just far enough away to clash with the sun so it forms a hard angle which is known as a square. Focus on the challenges you may be facing, be confident and know you're moving forward, making decisions that need to be made and working towards the manifestation of your dreams. Deal with anything that arises.

The Waxing Gibbous Moon – I found the word gibbous a strange one and had no idea what it meant when I first came across it, so checked out its meaning. It means convex, rounded or bulging.

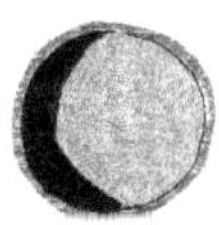

It's now the ideal time to be inspired, motivated and help your intention to grow. Finalise any plans which may have only been ideas until now – for instance, complete the application form for the job you've been thinking about, look at the detail of any contracts you're thinking of becoming involved with, get yourself into shape by joining the gym, that running group or yoga class. Take some positive action and build up some momentum towards the manifestation of your wish.

Stay on course with whatever you've started to put in motion with your wish. It's also a time when you can adjust your plans and ideas if you think there's a need.

Don't let fear or doubt spoil your wish. Stay open minded to what you're being taught by taking this journey and make any changes you need. Try not to get impatient or frustrated.

<u>The Full Moon</u> – It's during this phase of the moon that you can expect results. It's the time when things come to fruition - the time of manifestation. The moon's energy is at its highest, being the climax of the lunar cycle. Don't be surprised if strong emotions emerge and you're finding yourself on a short fuse and anxious, but also with far more energy than usual. You will find others to be exactly the same. Your body, which follows the moon's cycles, knows this is the climax of the moon cycle.

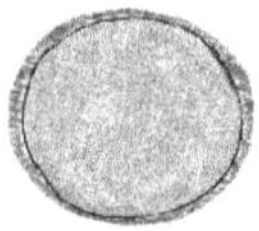

And so it's here. The moon's completely illuminated by the sun, giving us the full moon. If one of your wishes is to come true, it might manifest now as this is the time of completion. As I said earlier in this book, some wishes take time so you may simply get a sign that things are progressing. If this is the case, re-evaluate how you're feeling about what you wished for. Are you still happy with your wish and the plans you have put in motion? If something you wished for hasn't come to fruition, you may decide to let it go as full moon is also the time for release.

This is also the time to let go of any hurts since the last full moon and a time to forgive anyone who has hurt you in any way. It's not a time for blame. When you forgive, you can move forward - you release the karma and can leave a situation. It's also a time when emotions come to the surface, so do try to let go of any negative feelings you may be experiencing. A couple of key words to contemplate on or around the time of the full moon are forgiveness and gratitude. What do these words mean to you?

The full moon phase is also a lovely time to do some magic/spellwork. You might want to cast a spell to help you complete a task, for instance. It's a great time for divination, so you could try using your pendulum for any answers you're seeking, do a tarot card reading, scry your crystal ball or read the runes. It's also a good time to carry out a ritual and overall is a magical time to cast any spells relating to release and healing.

At the time of the full moon it's time to release your intention to the universe. You've spent time repeating and re-inforcing it since you set it at new moon. The universe knows what you want to manifest and you don't want to build up an attachment to it. So throw your arms in the air and really let go of your intention.

Without becoming too complex, you may like to try this simple way of celebrating the full moon. Place a glass of water in your garden or outside space at dusk so as the full moon rises, she can shine on your water. You might have a special glass, goblet or chalice you can use. At midnight go out and stand in the light of the moon. Honour her by raising your cup of moon/lunar energy charged water and see how you feel. Take a sip of the water and feel her energy. Even if you can't see the moon because of a cloudy sky, she's still there and you can absorb her energy and do this little ritual. Spend time bathing in the moonlight and allow it to nurture you.

<u>The Waning Gibbous Moon</u> – We're back to that word gibbous. This moon phase is seen for a couple of days after the full moon and you may also hear it being referred to as the disseminating moon.

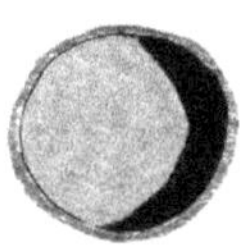

Now is the time to learn from any mistakes you've made; it's a time for letting go and for finishing off something. You might be wanting to give up a habit or an addiction – this is the time to do so. We're moving into the quieter time of the moon's cycle, a time where you should listen to your intuition and a time where your psychic powers heighten. The retreating lunar tide is here to sweep away the old, so this is why it's the perfect time for letting go, tying up loose ends, reflecting and learning any lessons.

So look after yourself and take time to rest. Tidy things up and de-clutter. You might want to try a releasing spell in terms of letting something go that no longer serves you. This moon phase is about ensuring a clean break is made with whatever might be bothering you so you can move forward. You may well find you have less energy and motivation, which is because the moon is now in the resting phase of her cycle. Use this time in the waning cycle to release anything that no longer serves your highest good.

Breathe, relax, regroup and accept what has happened. You might feel a bit flat that something hasn't worked out. Don't start anything new and go easy on yourself by accepting "what is". Simply down tools, take time to relax and enjoy some "me time".

The Third (or Last) Quarter - This is the third and last quarter of the moon. It's known by both names - and also as the waning half moon - and it appears as a half-moon facing in the opposite direction to the first quarter moon phase. It then decreases in size each night until its thin crescent finally disappears back into the light of the sun. Powers grow weaker so it's a time for rituals about closures and endings. Focus within yourself and look forward to what you'll be working with at the next new moon. Re-evaluate what has been happening and trust it's for the best. Now is the time to re-balance yourself if you've been feeling out of kilter with life.

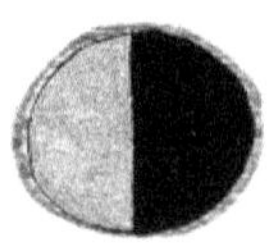

This moon phase is one of disintegration which continues until the dark moon (new moon phase). It can be a difficult time as it's at the half way point between the full and new moons so you might feel tired and a bit fraught. Are there any messages for you that emerge from any conflict and tension around you? You might want to give this some thought and may realise you need to change course. So the last quarter phase can be a time of finding yourself at a crossroads and possibly a time for some decision making.

<u>The Waning Crescent (or Balsamic) Moon</u> – There's something about this moon phase I just love and I look forward to it every lunar cycle. The name balsamic comes from the word "balsam", which means healing – and that's what this part of the lunar cycle is all about. It's a time of rest and renewal, so go easy on yourself and start to think about your dreams/wishes again. Be inspired and hopeful, enjoying your resting period.

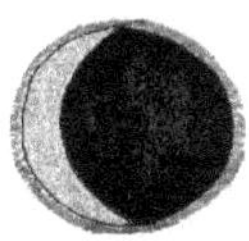

So what might you want to do during this moon phase? Research has shown it's a good time to cut your hair and nails if you don't want them to grow back too quickly - amazing what our lovely moon influences. It's also a good time to get into your garden and clear the weeds. But overall, just surrender to this lovely healing time. And so the lunar cycle is ending. It's time to let go and move on into the next lunar cycle that awaits you.

I do hope you have enjoyed this visitation through the lunar cycle and its phases and have learnt things that have taken me years to know, learn and understand. Now I want to touch on other aspects of the moon and "different" moons you may have heard about and need to be aware of. So let's continue with our journey.

The Void of Course Moon – Without going into a vast amount of astrological detail that complicates this, our Lady Moon completes her cycle via a revolution around the earth lasting about 28/29 days and passing through all 12 astrological signs, spending about 2-2.5 days in each – although this is very general. We'll be looking at the zodiac (astrological) signs in more detail soon, but in simple terms, the moon is void of course (usually identified on calendars as v/c) when she is passing from one sign to the next. This can take a few seconds or up to a couple of days. The moment the moon enters the new sign, the void of course period ends. I would strongly advise getting a moon diary (making sure it's in your time zone) and follow it day by day. I couldn't be without mine.

Void of course moons are a natural time for reflection and it's not a time to do any spellwork. Everything will simply fizzle out, so don't start anything during this period. What you might choose to do during this quieter moon time is take the opportunity to be productive on any projects you've got underway and to which you want to give your undivided attention. From experience, things do get a bit quieter during the void of course, so it's a good time to meditate and slip away to other realms.

As already mentioned, during this time please remember to avoid anything new, including new purchases. Avoid any important communications - don't sign any contracts and don't do any spell work. It's a great time to meditate, clean your house, relax, sleep, read a book and be with people without any expectation from them. This is how I remember what the void of course moon means – have no expectations from anyone or anything.

However, on the other hand, if you're anxious about doing something because of a reaction you may receive, the void of course moon could be the perfect time to take the plunge and do whatever you need to do. It's unlikely you'll get the reaction you're anticipating.

If you start something during the void of course moon, it's highly likely to fail, so please don't start anything new that really matters to you as it won't be successful.

The Super Moon – This happens when the full moon coincides with the moon's closest approach to earth in its orbit. Super moons make the moon appear a little brighter and closer to the earth than normal giving the effect that it's bigger. They cause higher than usual tides which is down to the force of gravity on the earth.

So a super moon equates to supercharged full moon energies. When the energy is used correctly, it can be an immensely positive experience and be a very beneficial moon, but may also lead to emotional turmoil with old dramas re-surfacing, revealing some lower vibrational energies. So, do take care.

Blue Moon – A blue moon is the name for the second full moon in a calendar month, although there is a more complex astronomical interpretation which I won't worry you with. It's relatively rare, hence where the expression "once in a blue moon" comes from. Without going into too much detail, the blue moon has an impact on the new and full moons and the astrological signs are out of sync for a while but do gradually adjust again.

We can all use the energy of a blue moon to focus our intentions and get a better understanding of ourselves. This knowledge can then be used to help pull together a more positive future.

Black Moon – This is also fairly rare and refers to the second new moon in a calendar month so it's a second chance to set your intention in the same month.

Blood Moon – This refers to the reddish tinge a full moon takes on when there's been a total lunar eclipse.

Eclipses of the moon – These occur when the moon passes behind the earth and moves into the earth's shadow. It happens approximately 3 times a year on the night of a new or full moon. A new moon eclipse is called a solar eclipse and a full moon eclipse is a lunar eclipse. You may well have heard the term "eclipse season" to describe a series of eclipses.

In the past, our ancestors feared eclipses – the sky grew dark, birds stopped singing, dogs stopped barking and everyone was terrified, blaming anything negative that happened on the eclipses as an eerie silence covered the earth. Today eclipses are viewed in a far more positive light and considered to be portents of change. A solar eclipse symbolises a dramatic new beginning and a lunar eclipse supercharges the energy of the full moon.

Eclipses are generally used to harness some "good luck". For example, you might want to make a talisman (see Appendix 3) during this time and carry it with you – perhaps if you're taking a driving test or going for an interview.

Chapter 4 - The Sun's Energy (Solar Energy)

I imagine you're pretty familiar with the fact the sun passes through all 12 astrological signs during the course of the year, remaining in each for approximately a month. I think of this movement through each sign as the solar energy that affects all of us. Its pace is far slower than the energy of the moon as the moon moves through each astrological sign during its 28/29 day cycle.

The sun is the essential source of life giving energy for our planet, Mother Earth. People have always recognised a connection between the sun and life here on earth. It's hardly surprising that worshipping the sun was such a common feature of spiritual life in many cultures and/or religions. Throughout history, the words "energy" and "power" have also been used to describe spiritual forces (as well as the sun) and for some of them, this will also have included a god or goddess of the sun (or many of each).

Today we know that solar energy is radiant white light and the heat from the sun is employed on earth by using a range of technologies such as solar heating, solar thermal energy and molten salt power plants. In the same vein, sun gods and goddesses were considered to be invincible and as powerful as the sun itself.

A sun (or solar) god represented the sun or any aspect of the sun, such as heat or fire. There are also some sun goddesses, but for the purposes of my book, I'm only referring to sun gods and moon goddesses, so the male and female energies can be clearly delineated. A sun god was usually considered to be powerful, courageous and strong, words associated with the masculine energy.

Most sun gods are depicted as looking human, riding or driving some kind of vessel across the sky - such as a boat, chariot or even a cup. The sun gave light and life and was considered to be a source of wisdom. As an example, the sun god in Hinduism, who was called Surya, travelled across the sky in a chariot pulled by either seven horses - or a single seven-headed horse - and he fought darkness.

There may be more than one god of the sun that was worshipped. For instance, the Egyptians differentiated between the various aspects of the sun and had several sun gods – one was associated with the rising sun, one with the setting sun and one with the midday sun. The Greeks and Romans also had more than one sun god.

The Celts sun god was Lugh, who was revered at the Lammas festival in what Wiccans call the Wheel of the Year. The Wheel of the year is an annual cycle of festivals which link to important turning points in the agricultural calender celebrated by modern day pagans - and there's more about this later in my book.

I've listed a few of the sun gods that you may want to incorporate in your work with energies. Of course, you can research this and find others that may resonate with you. You'll also find out the link between the solar journey and earth energy in the chapter about the Wheel of the Year festivals.

Helios, a Greek sun god before Apollo.
Apollo, who was the Greek sun god after Helios and drove a sun chariot.
Surya, a Hindu sun god who rode a horse-drawn chariot through the sky.
Lugh, a Celtic god who was celebrated at Lammas (or Lughnasadh).
Ra, an Egyptian sun god who had a solar disc over his head.

Sun worship has always been associated with the pagan religion but almost every culture/religion uses solar associations. All these cultures/religions had well developed communities with strong ideas about sun worship. The sun represented power, justice, strength and wisdom, which was central to their worship. So sun energy became very important. Kings were believed to be ruled by the power of the sun - so the sun was considered to be the supreme god.

As an example, the ancient Egyptians honoured a sun god called Ra. Their temples were built with an opening at the top, so the sun rays could pour down on the altar to provide spiritual energy for their worship. For those who follow the pagan pathway, rituals relating to the sun traditionally occur in June at the time of the Summer Solstice (or Litha). This is the time of the year when the sun reaches its highest position in the sky and is the longest day of the year. Groups gather together to celebrate with food, drumming and dancing until the sun goes down.

So now with a bit more knowledge about solar energy, its impact on cultures and religions and the sun's annual movement through the astrological signs, we'll start to explore how the energy of these signs impact on working with our Lady Moon. We'll move on to learn about what each astrologicial sign represents and how you can use your knowledge to enhance your work through the lunar cycle.

Chapter 5 - The Astrological/Sun Signs

Lunar influence has always been central to the study of astrology world-wide. The moon is linked to the feminine, the mother figure and to our emotions. As previously mentioned, she moves from one sign to the next one approximately every 2.5 days presenting new experiences and changes in our behaviour depending on the astrological sign the moon finds herself in. I'll expand on this shortly as we work through this chapter. For instance, if the moon is in Taurus, you might find yourself and others being more stubborn; if in Leo, more dramatic and self-centred; if in Sagittarius, more optimistic and adventurous and if in Scorpio, more secretive and suspicious.

In addition to the knowledge you've now gained about the lunar cycle and the moon's phases through the cycle, the moon is intrinsically linked to solar energy by its movement through the astrological/sun signs, which we're going to be exploring. Many of you may not realise the importance of astrological signs in relation to the moon and your only experience of them may be reading your horoscope. By recognising the astrological sign the moon is in will help you work with the moon far more effectively and I hope this chapter will expand your knowledge.

I've focussed on the new moon when writing about the impact of the signs, but equally they have the same associations during the other moon phases, although the effect of the ever changing phases is different. The new moon is about new beginnings, a new start, the time to plant a seed - and a time to set an intention around any new projects or plans you have.

We start with Aries as this is where the astrological year begins and will work our way through the year giving an idea of each of the sign's energy and what you can use it for.

Aries – "I am" ♈ Aries' element is fire and there's some very fiery energy attached to this sign. It's a time when you can feel impulsive, enthusiastic, determined and energetic. So be aware when the moon is in Aries, that for a couple of days everyone may be more aggressive, impatient, stressed or argumentative. Competition's in the air and you may find yourself having to be more assertive than you might need to be normally. Things around you happen quickly, but things also pass just as quickly. As it's the first sign of the zodiac, it's a great time to start new projects. Aries is the leader of the astrological new year and full of confidence. If you're wanting to start a project around having more courage, winning or being more assertive, this is the perfect time to get your wishes underway.

Taurus – "I have" ♉ This sign's element is earth with a solid, stable energy, feeling secure and well rooted. Its energy is about the ability to nurture (including finances), being confident in what you're doing - and is a sensual energy. There's no point rushing about or changing anything – everything's fine just as it is. If you want to start something that's meant to last, this is a great time to take action. So it's a good time to make wishes under the new moon in Taurus connected to money, property and possessions in some way – for example, buying a house. Additionally, it's a positive time to do some work around your self-esteem, confidence and your sensuality.

Gemini – "I know" ♊ Gemini's element is air, so there may well be lots of movement and chattering around you. There's a restless feel to the energy, plus lots of lively exchanges taking place. Some problem solving could also be occurring. Now isn't the time for making commitments as you can't expect promises made under the influence of the Gemini energy to be kept. Things started now are easily changed by outside influences. So, it's a time for wishes around being clear with someone, expressing yourself, starting to write a book – and is also a great time to communicate with others or to sit down and read a good book.. The Gemini new moon is all about creating better communication.

Cancer – "I feel" ♋ Just the expression "I feel" implies Cancer has water as its element, which of course it does. It's all about expressing our emotions and is a warm, nurturing sign, relating to protection and our maternal instincts. It's concerned with our homes and family. Cancer's typical reactions are sympathy, empathy, understanding plus caring for others – doing the cooking, cleaning and washing. So in terms of how the moon in Cancer may affect you, it can be an emotional time – watch out for becoming moody or over-sensitive. It's also the time to take care of your domestic issues – perhaps you're thinking about buying a new home, building better relationships with particular family members, re-decorating your home or buying a new dishwasher. This is the time to wish for them – right under the Cancer new moon.

Leo – "I create" ♌ Leo's element is fire, so prepare for some drama to be around you. As with other fire signs, this can be a fiery time. Everyone around you appears to be needing recognition and appreciation and of course, this might even be you. Lots of excitement is about, with the negative side being that it can all turn rather dramatic. When no drama's around, it's a creative, spontaneous and fun loving time. Leo focuses on "me" and away from others and their emotional needs. The energy can be fast paced, flamboyant and dynamic. When working with the new moon in Leo, you might want to set an intention about being more generous as Leo is the sign of generosity.

Virgo – "I analyse" ♍ Virgo's element is earth. Time to pay attention to your diet, hygiene, health and think about how you use your time. If you want to break a habit, Virgo energy is the one to work with to get things going. Focus on what's important in your life as well as what might need fixing. It's a time for decision making, some honest reflection, taking care of things, getting organised and helping others. Virgo's known as the most helpful of all signs, often neglecting themselves and wanting to be of service. If you want to work with the Virgo energy, make magic around being more helpful to someone in your life or being punctual, reliable and organised - or you might have decided you need to be disciplined about getting into better shape, losing weight or eating more healthily. This is the sign to wish and plan under.

Libra – "I relate" ♎ Libra's element is air. Now our attention turns to our partners, our relationships and the sharing of our experiences. Its astrological symbol is the scales, giving a clear message that Libra is about restoring balance in our lives. It's a time to co-operate, negotiate and compromise if there's a need. Libran energy is sociable, polite and friendly. If you're one for lots of social activities, this energy is a good time to enjoy your socialising and friendships, so arrange a get together. Use the new moon in Libra for better relationships with others – perhaps by setting an intention to be a better partner or a more reliable friend to someone. In fact, you can use this energy to make intentions about any relationships you have to enable a more balanced and harmonious approach in your life.

Scorpio – "I desire" ♏ A deeply emotional sign with its element obviously being water. It's the most intense sign experiencing strong emotions, whether we consider those emotions positive or negative. So feelings such as passion, jealousy, betrayal, love, revenge, happiness and desire are all emphasised when the moon is in the sign of Scorpio. The Scorpio new moon is a very powerful time and emotions may be experienced to the point of being obsessive. You may find yourself becoming secretive, suspicious or stewing over something that others find completely irrelevant. It's also a time of increased awareness of your psychic ability. So, under this new moon you might be making wishes around sex or money – both being emotional topics. It's also a good time to get to the bottom of something, to find out a secret or to take control of an aspect of your life.

Sagittarius – "I understand" ♐ Sagittarius is the last of the astrological signs in the astrological year whose element is fire. It has the most optimistic, non-judgemental, adventurous and positive energy of all the sun signs. It's time to shake off any grudges you may have been holding on to and turn things around. When the moon's in Sagittarius, it's simply time to "chill out" and relax. It's a good time to take off somewhere you've never been, have a new experience or learn something new. It's the sign of the adventurer and is very spontaneous. If you want to work with this energy, then make wishes about having fun, learning to relax and lighten up a bit. It's also a time to make commitments about where to go, what to do and with whom.

Capricorn – "I utilise" ♑ The final earth sign in the astrological year. Capricorn's the most practical and business-like of all the sun signs. Under its energy, feelings will be expressed in an organised, unemotional way. This energy brings out the duty in all of us as we focus on our obligations and responsibilities. There's a desire to work rather than play and our focus is on becoming more responsible. Plans and goals become all important, so use this time to work on your business affairs, organise a part of your life that has become disorganised, write a to do list and action it. Set out some guidelines to help you keep focused in the future. Wishes under the Capricorn new moon should focus on your work/career/projects and what you're wanting to achieve from them.

Aquarius –"I change" ♒ The Aquarian element is air and the last of the air sun signs in the zodiac. It's time for some inspiration in your world – a time to do something outrageous or eccentric and break the rules. Aquarius represents the rebel, breaking from the past and everything that's come to restrict us. So how about some personal freedom and saying no to all the rules that are in place? This energy helps us break free from our routines, rules and habits so we become more unique. You'll find that erratic, extreme and abrupt actions take place under the Aquarian moon and things appear more unpredictable than usual. If you want to make some wishes under the Aquarian new moon, consider which area in your life needs to move forward and how you might go about getting there. This is a detached new moon so it won't be a time when you get overly emotional about anything as the energy is quite isolated.

Pisces – "I believe" ♓ Pisces is the last sun sign in the astrological year and its element is water. It's a time to rest, to sleep, to meditate, to wish. It's an emotional moon when boundaries may well disappear. We might seem vague, nostalgic and vulnerable. The energy of the Pisces moon is also the most spiritual time – it's a time to do a ritual or spell and to meditate. You may also find yourself being more intuitive, sensitive and empathetic under this sun sign. When working with the Piscean energy, you could make a commitment to your spiritual life – for instance, you might decide to commit to meditating every day or starting to learn to use your tarot cards.

Fixed, Cardinal and Mutable sun signs

Before we proceed any further, it's also worth knowing that all the astrological signs are categorised into either fixed, cardinal or mutable groups and there are four astrological signs in each group. This basically explains the different ways in which you interact and engage with others. There's no right or wrong. This affects everything you do - from how you approach your to-do list, deal with change in your life and even approach your social life. It's worth considering these "qualities" when thinking about which moon sign you should do your wish or spellwork with.

Cardinal Signs - ***Aries, Cancer, Libra, Capricorn***

These four signs start each of our seasons......Aries = spring (and the start of the zodiac), Cancer = summer, Libra = autumn and Capricorn = winter. As this implies, they are the initiators of the zodiac – the leaders who have all the ideas and initiate that first energy of a project or an idea. They're creative with a desire to be first at everything. They constantly think about new and fresh ways to approach any situation. They're the entrepreneurs; the ones who get things going; initiating action and often the centre of attention.

On the other hand, there will often be a lack of action and follow through. They struggle making plans a reality and can also get frustrated and potentially aggressive when others don't immediately jump on board with their ideas.

Fixed Signs - ***Taurus, Leo, Scorpio, Aquarius***

These four signs fall in the middle of every season.....Taurus = spring, Leo = summer, Scorpio = autumn and Aquarius = winter. They're the ones who build the foundations of a project and start the building work. They're the ones who keep the initial energy going that's already been created by the cardinal signs.They pick up their ideas, turning them into reality. They're trustworthy and work from their "to-do" lists. "Fixed" energy is about stability – they're your patient, steady workers.

This "fixed" energy is very driven and focused. It tends to be more predictable than the other astrological signs. Once a fixed sign puts something in motion - whether it's a project or a relationship – they stick with it. However, this energy resists change and has difficulty opening up to different opinions and ideas. So it can be a stubborn energy not liking any change and appearing inflexible.

Mutable Signs - ***Gemini, Virgo, Sagittarius, Pisces***
These four signs end each season – Gemini = spring; Virgo = summer; Sagittarius = autumn and Pisces = winter. They're very aware all good things come to an end, so their role is to prepare everyone for this. They're far more flexible and comfortable with change than the cardinal or fixed signs and easily adapt and are known for their wisdom. They're often the ones who complete projects/plans for the other signs. The mutable signs "go with the flow".

They're flexible and able to change quickly so can adapt to any situation or person relatively easily. They're the open-minded signs of the zodiac who understand and accept differences of opinion as they can change their style to fit in. However, their ability to change can often leave them feeling energetically low at times and they can have trouble sorting through their own emotions, thoughts and decisions which gives them difficulties.

Chapter 6 - Working with Associations

These are some tips I've learnt to use when working with the lunar cycle, along with the moon and sun energies. I'm not saying it's imperative to use these, but I believe you'll find them beneficial to your workings and they do enhance your practice. Nothing is cast in stone, so if some of these resonate with you, try them and see what works. If they don't, then leave them alone.

Working with the moon phase at different times of the day

When you're working with the moon in whatever phase, whether that's the new moon when you're setting your intention (Chapter 7) or doing some forgiveness and release work during other moon phases, below are the best times I've found to do your ritual/ spell work to maximum benefit.

Dawn – do spells around employment, your career or business - as well as studying, healing and travelling.

During the day – if an issue in your life means standing up to someone, or having to deal with some difficult "male" issues - you might want to choose the daylight hours to do your work. You can then draw on the sun's energy in your work, which is the masculine energy.

Noon – do spells around being successful, being courageous and strong, finances and protection.

Dusk/sunset – the best time to do spells to help solve a problem, such as getting over a relationship, a job loss or a time of grief in your life – so a time to find resolution to something. It's a good time to set your intention for a new beginning away from your problems. Also it's the time for spells around health, releasing anything that you've failed at, banishing any emotional pain and upset.

Night – do your work when the moon is visible to you – or you know she's there behind the clouds. The best spells to do at this time may involve "female" issues, plus intuitive and psychic work which might include some divination. Also it's the time for rituals and spells to enhance your development, release old wounds and to release any stress.

However, of course, the best time to do your moon work will always be when you're wide awake, alert and full of energy to maintain your focus. Other tips might be using the weather or elements (see chapter 10) as part of your work – for example, you might work on a cold winter's day to freeze someone – or their behaviour – out of your life. Or you may choose to work on the nearest new moon to one of the Wheel of the Year festivals – so if you want to bring love or romance into your life, you may decide to do a love spell on the nearest new moon to Beltane (more about the Wheel of the Year in Chapter 9).

How to amplify and enhance your wishes/spells/magic/dreams/intentions

With every moon phase there are many associations – colours, planets, herbs, astrological signs (which we've already covered), days of the week, crystals, essential oils and so on. I'm only giving you an overview as this is a vast subject in itself but I'll guide you with what I know works from my experience. Using these suggestions in your work will amplify your magical workings.

Monday ☽ - governed by the moon, so wishes/spells/rituals today would be about female energy, beauty, wisdom, peace, healing, caring, psychic awareness, spirituality and purification;

Tuesday ♂ - governed by Mars, so wishes/spells/rituals today would be about being courageous, protection, warding off negativity, passion, aggression and sexuality;

Wednesday ☿ - governed by Mercury, so wishes/spells/rituals today would be about communication, luck, creativity, study and travel;

Thursday ♃ - governed by Jupiter, so wishes/spells/rituals today would be about money, health, fertility, expansion and generosity;

Friday ♀ - governed by Venus, so wishes/spells/rituals today would be about love, romance, reconciliation, relationships and friendships;

Saturday ♄ - governed by Saturn, so wishes/spells/rituals today would be about wisdom, psychic stuff, magic, endings, release and your home;

Sunday ☉ - governed by the sun, so wishes/spells/rituals today would be linked to masculine energy, self-confidence, success, strength and protection.

When making a wish or performing a spell or ritual on a particular day of the week, you might want to enhance it by having some crystals around that are associated with the day and the planet that rules the day. You may also want to place objects of a particular colour around your working space (or altar), a vase with a small posy of associated tree leaves or flowers – whatever suits you. Each day of the week also has a metal associated with it and you might choose to have a symbol made from it. There are also herbs, plants and essential oils associated with each day. Below is my list of what you can work with - I should just state this list isn't exhaustive, but they're my personal choices. You may choose not to do this at all. That's also fine. This path is about what works for you and what you feel comfortable with.

Monday
Crystals = pearl, moonstone
Colours = silver, black, white, pale blue
Tree = willow
Flowers = lily, jasmine, bluebell
Metal = silver
Plant/herb = chamomile
Essential oils = jasmine, lily, sandalwood.

Tuesday
Crystals = bloodstone, garnet
Colours = red, black
Tree = holly
Flowers = geranium, snapdragon, thistle
Metal = iron
Plant/herb = ginger, garlic, peppers
Essential oils = pine, ginger, basil.

Wednesday
Crystals = opal, agate
Colours = violet/purple, orange
Tree = hazel
Flowers = lily of the valley, lavender
Metal = quicksilver, mercury
Plant/herb = lavender, dill
Essential oils = lavender, bergamot, eucalyptus.

Thursday
Crystals = amethyst, turquoise
Colours = blue, purple, green, turquoise
Tree = oak
Flowers = carnation, honeysuckle
Metal = tin
Plant/herb = cinnamon, nutmeg
Essential oils = clove, sage, peppermint.

Friday
Crystals = emerald, rose quartz
Colours = green, pink, coral
Tree = apple
Flowers = rose, geranium
Metal = copper
Plant/herb = strawberry
Essential oils = geranium, ylang ylang, rose.

Saturday
Crystals = onyx, black obsidian, black tourmaline, haematite
Colours = black, blue, indigo, grey, brown
Tree = alder
Flowers = jasmine, pansy
Metal = lead
Plant/herb = thyme, pomegranate
Essential oils = cypress, myrrh, patchouli, vetiver.

Sunday
Crystals = topaz, amber, carnelian
Colours = gold, yellow, orange
Tree = bay
Flowers = sunflower, marigold
Metal = gold
Plant/herb = orange, cinnamon
Essential oils = cinnamon, orange, bergamot.

<u>Oils to use with each astrological sign and their ruling plants</u>
When the moon is in a particular astrological sign you're wanting to work with, you can also work with the essential oil of that sign rather than the essential oil associated with the day of the week.

So as a quick reference, here are the signs with their associated ruling planet(s) plus the oils you might choose to use for your magic making.

Aries – governed by Mars – rosemary, lavender or bergamot
Taurus – governed by Venus – rose, sandalwood or frankincense
Gemini – governed by Mercury – basil, clary sage or rose
Cancer – governed by the Moon - blue chamomile, sandalwood or cinnamon
Leo – governed by the Sun – jasmine, bergamot or ylang ylang
Virgo – governed by Mercury – lavender, peppermint or cedarwood
Libra – governed by Venus – geranium, rose or marjoram
Scorpio – governed by Pluto/Mars – patchouli, ginger or lemon
Sagittarius – governed by Jupiter - black pepper or rosewood
Capricorn – governed by Saturn – vetiver or lemon
Aquarius – governed by Uranus – neroli, marjoram or cinnamon
Pisces – governed by Neptune/Jupiter – melissa, cinnamon or fennel

Additional Associations

Depending on your views, you may like to consider whether to include having any representations of any goddesses/gods (deities) associated with the days of the week around you when you're making your magic. These could be in picture form – you might find one that encompasses what you feel is the energy of that day of the week – or a picture of the deity that you can easily find on the internet. Alternatively, you can buy statues off the internet or in mystical shops if that's your preference. I believe their "presence" can enhance the work you're doing.

If you work with tarot cards, you can also include them in your work. My suggestions for both deities and tarot cards are below:

Monday
Deity = Selene, Thoth
Tarot cards = Moon, High Priestess, High Priest/Heirophant

Tuesday
Deity = Lilith, Mars
Tarot cards = Strength, 6 of Wands
Wednesday
Deity = Athena, Mercury
Tarot cards = Magician, Wheel of Fortune
Thursday
Deity = Juno, Thor
Tarot cards = Ace of Pentacles, 10 of Pentacles
Friday
Deity = Aphrodite, Eros
Tarot cards = Empress, Lovers
Saturday
Deity = Hecate, Saturn
Tarot cards = Temperance, Knight of Swords
Sunday
Deity = Brighid, Helios
Tarot cards = Sun, Ace of Wands

Additionally, if you're working with particular phases of the moon, you can work with the following goddesses:

New moon – Juna, Maeve
Waxing moon – Zirna, Artemis
Full moon – Demeter
Waning moon - Hecate

There are other moon goddesses, so choose the one that feels right for you.

Chapter 7 - Setting Your Intention

Creating lunar abundance is helped positively by the use of intention. So, what is an intention? It's what you intend the outcome of your wish/spell to be, which needs to be clear, focused and always in the present tense as though you're already living your dream. So here's a bit more information about the lunar cycle/energy before we get into the detail of intention setting.

A bit of knowledge about the yin and yang energies, which are widely used in Chinese medicine, can also be useful when you're working with the moon. The yin energy lunar phases are a time for listening, restoring, reflecting, just "being" and receiving. It's the feminine energy, the time of darkness and depth. The yang energy lunar phases are about initiating, action, doing and giving - they're all about masculine energy, which is less dense than the feminine yin energy, about activity and moving forward.

However, you may have noticed a theme in this book and that is we all need a balance of energies in our lives – this includes both these energies to create harmony within ourselves. In order to create more harmony, when you're working with the moon phases, you might want to take note about which are ruled by yin and which by yang energy. Again, it's up to you whether you choose to use these.

Yin Moon Phases (female energy)

Waxing crescent moon

Go within as this phase gives you some time to slow down and reflect on how you're really feeling. Ask yourself where you need to slow down in your life – and do so. Be ready to receive.

Waxing gibbous moon

Just trust in the divine – and trust in yourself and take time to stop. Ask spirit how you can be more trusting of others and for help with this. Don't let anxiety get the better of you. Evaluate your progress. Do some journaling and meditation – any activities you love that take your focus away from problems.

Waning gibbous or disseminating moon

Time to be grateful for what you've received and really appreciate it. Become consciously aware of any changes that have taken place and be thankful for anything that has reached fruition.

Balsamic or waning crescent moon

This phase is about the return to darkness and a time for reflection. Reflect on any lessons you've learnt since the new moon. It's sometimes a challenging time as it's the ending of the moon cycle. Be grateful, appreciative, reflective, relax and re-charge.

Yang Moon Phases (male energy)

New moon

The time of planting the seed for something you're wanting to manifest if your life. The time of new beginnings and some action. What do you want to achieve or express? Set your intention, which can be as simple as you want it to be – and really believe it will happen.

First quarter moon or waxing half-moon

Back to reality and time to take some action in support of your intention. Become determined about what you're wanting to manifest in your life by being pro-active in your planning and working out your priorities.

Full moon
Your intention might come to fruition now. However, it may be some time before this happens – or it may not happen. Be proud of what you've achieved so far. Be aware of your emotional reactions at the full moon and take any corrective action that's needed to put any issues right. Think what/who you need to forgive so you can release and heal. Be grateful and appreciative.

Third (or last) quarter moon or waning half moon
Time to reach out to others in your world, being kind and giving towards them. Be generous and share what you've been given. This phase is about giving back. Take more care of yourself and have some "me time".

To note:
Always spend some time at the end of every lunar cycle to reflect on what has happened during it. Be grateful for anything that was successful since the last new moon as gratitude is a wonderful way to attract more into your life.

<u>Setting your intentions at the new moon</u>
Casting your intentions, wishes or spells are carried out in the main to change your life for the better.

However, it's not as simple as that. For instance, if you're wishing for more love in your life, you need to give out more love in some way. This is the Law of Attraction, another subject far too vast for this little book but something you can research if you're interested. There are also many good books on this topic.

It's also important not to try to influence anyone's free will, so if your intention is around a particular person, you'll need to include that it should also be right for that person as well as for yourself. This ensures you've no selfish motive.

Don't be mechanical with your magic - there are hundreds of spell books telling you what you should be saying, what you should be doing and what props/tools to use. As I've said several times throughout the writing of this book, it must be right for you. It's not just about saying and doing what a book tells you, but about what resonates with you as a person and your intention has to be for the highest good of all.

From experience through my many years of practice, I've bought a book, read it from cover to cover, digested it word for word, have done exactly as it's told me for my spells - and I've waited... and waited.... and waited for a result. The result was nothing – and that may well be a result – but my point is I was doing things robotically as the book stated. This would then lead me to discard the book and go and buy what I considered to be a better book. Same story.

Eventually it dawned on me that I had to make any work that I did mine. My magic had to be owned by me and energetically charged by me. Once I realised this and could fully understand and believe in myself, making up my own spells and using the various associations that I'd come to learn, things began to change. Of course, I now have a wonderful array of books, which I still refer to if needed, but my workings are owned by me. The important point about this is that your own energy needs to be projected into your intention. And the work doesn't just stop once you've set your intention; it has to be re-affirmed numerous times and believed in throughout.

We need to spend time altering our state of consciousness before setting any intention. This is done through grounding and protecting ourselves, meditating, visualising, casting a circle, chanting, dancing and/or drumming. Your own energy and emotions are then added to this.

Spells/wishes come from your heart and not your head. Without feelings and energy involved, they're unlikely to come to fruition. So, before moving on, the real power of any spell work is within you - that intrinsically includes your connection with spirit, the goddess, higher self/consciousness, divinity, angels, your guides – whatever you call it - and when you understand the true nature of energy, you can make wishes about your future become reality - with the right intention, of course. We need to remember everything is energy and therefore everything is connected.

Preparation Prior to Intention Setting

There are several different ways in which you can prepare to set your intention. You might want to use just one – you might want to mix and match any of these suggestions. Or you might not want to use any of these and do further looking around to find a way to prepare that best suits you – but you must prepare yourself to work with the spiritual realms.

(a) One way in which to prepare to set your intention is by creating a vision board where you put your energy into the things that you want to manifest in your life. The idea behind it is that you surround yourself with images of what you want to have or do in the future by placing those images on the board and adding any positive thoughts or words to it.

You'll need to buy a canvas board – these are easily available from any craft shop or off the internet and are in various sizes. You'll also need a pile of magazines, some glue, scissors and anything you might want to decorate your vision board with – stickers, craft tape, crystals, glitter, etc. To enhance the energy you are putting in, you might also want to add a photo of yourself in the centre of the board and then surround yourself with pictures of what you want to achieve. Or place it in the middle of the board at the bottom and put your pictures above your photo in the shape of a fan.

In order to make your vision board, firstly go through your magazines, tearing out images from them and making a pile in front of you. Enjoy looking through them, pulling out any pictures, words or headlines that mean something to you. When your pile is complete, go back through the images and words, use your intuition and place your favourite pictures on your board. In addition, there might be something you particularly want but can't find in the magazines you have, so research it on the internet and print off its image.

Think about the layout of your board. You might decide on a theme for each corner of the board - health, career/job, spirituality, relationships, finances, home. Then start cutting and gluing everything onto your board.

Add your own writing if you wish, which enhances your personal energy. Really make it yours. Add stickers and other decorations. Lastly, when you've completed your vision board and are happy with it, put it in a place where you will see it every day.

(b) An idea similar to a vision board is a vision journal. It could be you don't want others in your home to see your wishes, so this is a more private way of preparing for intention setting. It uses similar principles as vision boarding, but in a book. So you might want to buy a book containing plain paper and keep an on-going vision journal, sticking in relevant pictures and phrases as they appear.

(c) Another way to prepare is to have a "sacred" bath before sending your intention/wishes to the universe. These have been used in every ancient culture as part of any ritual. You'll be amazed how creative your mind can become and the guidance and inspiration you may receive. There are all kinds of sacred ritual baths – for success, wisdom, emotional balance, increasing self-esteem, banishing worry or attracting money, along with many more.

So, for instance, if your intention is about bringing some love into your life, you might choose rose essential oil in your bath, adding a rose quartz or moonstone crystal and lighting a red or pink candle. You may even float some rose petals on the water.

(d) If the idea of taking a sacred bath doesn't appeal to you, then I really believe in a bath or shower being a pre-curser to doing any spell/wish work. It divides your daily activities from your magical activities. So light a candle in the bathroom, include some Epsom salts in your bath with some essential oil. If your preference is to shower, then if you use liquid soap, add a drop or two of essential oil to it. Focus on washing away the energies of the day and visualise them going down the plughole. Mix some essential oil with a carrier oil and rub it into your skin after bathing or showering. You could select an oil that matches your intention or the astrological sign you're going to be working under - and might choose an appropriate coloured candle to burn, although white is always fine.

(e) Another option – and one that always works for me – is to do some meditation work. Meditation clears your mind but – again – is something to be practised. These things don't just happen. During meditation we can ground and protect ourselves and create a peaceful space, training ourselves to be present in the "now". Our minds are constantly chattering away as we go through our busy lives and meditation helps slow this down – and eventually erase it. It masters mind over matter and helps you focus.

In addition, all the energies we pick up during our daily life need to be cleansed before you step into working with the spiritual realms (Chapter 12). Making a division between your everyday life and spellcasting puts you in the right mind-set for intention setting.

Intention Setting

So now you've done your preparation, space/energy cleansing and it's time to be clear on what you're wanting to manifest in your life. You will, of course, already have some ideas about this, but I find it helpful to ask myself some questions so I'm clear on my real focus, which is sometimes not what I expect it to be. These questions are initially along the lines of:

- What do I want to achieve?
- Why do I want to achieve this? What is my motive?
- Who is going to benefit?
- When do I want this to happen?

Then dive deeper to other areas of your life that you might want to think about and question, such as:

- Where do I live? Am I happy here? What improvements do I want to make?
- What work do I do? Do I want to change my job/go for promotion? Do I want to set up my own business?
- What are my relationships like? Consider work colleagues, friends and family. What has been my contribution to these relationships?
- What is my health/diet/exercise regime like?
- What does my bank account look like? Am I living to my limits with nothing to spare? Am I being too frugal with what I've been given?
- How am I spiritually? Do I commit enough time to spiritual development?

More questions will come to you as you think about what you're wanting to achieve - and always be honest in your answers and reflections. Write down all your thoughts.

So now it's the new moon and time to set your intention. Check the astrological sign in which the new moon is occurring as this can also benefit your manifesting. The way in which you set your intention may be similar to the following mini ritual:

1. Find a quiet space at home or outside where you're not likely to be disturbed. You may already have a designated sacred space. Cast your circle (Chapter 12). Light some candles and play some meditative music to help create a relaxing atmosphere. Choose to diffuse an essential oil if you're inside. If you're outside, take your oil with you, rubbing a couple of drops of it into your palms and breathing it in for a few minutes. Use all the associations – or just one of them – as outlined in Chapter 6.

2. Make yourself comfortable. Relax and close your eyes, taking some deep breaths. Focus on what you feel would enhance your life. You'll have already spent time thinking about your intention, so visualise being where you want to be – or enjoying whatever it is you wish to have. You might want to hold either a selenite or celestite crystal during this quiet time as these crystals are a link to the spiritual realms.

3. When you're ready, open your eyes and write down what you've been thinking about or what images you may have seen – setting your intention. You might want to draw a picture rather than writing, but it's very important your intention is drawn/written by you so it's imbued with your energy. While you were reflecting, did anything come to you to show you whether you might want to do something extra to achieve what you're intending? If so, you might want to add something in your intention about it. As a reminder, ensure your intention is in the present tense as if you've already received it.

4. You should also ask for help from the spiritual realms in achieving your intention whilst writing it down. At this point

it may be that you have no idea how it might manifest, but don't worry about that. Close down your circle (Chapter 12).

5. So now your intention is set. Refer to it on a daily basis – even if you only have five minutes a day to do so, it's a positive affirmation of what you want to manifest. Work with your intention every day throughout the lunar cycle. State it aloud if you can as this enhances its power.

6. You might also choose to fold up the paper on which you've written your intention and keep it in a small pouch or bag. You could add a clear quartz crystal to heighten spiritual awareness along with something that represents your desires, such as rose petals for love or a small silver coin for prosperity. Put it under your pillow before sleeping and ask for messages in your dreams which could help you fulfil your intention.

As an example of an intention that was successful for me – some time ago when I was feeling I wanted to learn more about crystals and their properties, my intention was along the lines of "I am in tune with the therapeutic power of crystals and am helping myself and others". A goal I set myself a few years ago so I could manifest this was to attend a crystal therapy course, although at the time I had no idea who even ran such a course or if I could afford it. A course eventually came along and now I use crystals in all my work, either when I give treatments, hold a ritual/circle or run an esoteric training course. They're a permanent part of my life.

I hope these ideas and suggestions have lit a spark within you to start practising what feels right and works for you.

Chapter 8 - Some More Moon Info

Here are a few random pieces of information you may have had questions about, so I hope these snippets of information explain things.

Covens

You may have heard of these under a number of different titles – a gathering, a moot, a sisterhood, a moon group, a circle - whatever the name and however it's disguised (rather like the name "spell" has become "wish" to become more socially acceptable) these names are all referring to people who meet to connect with lunar energy. So these covens (or whatever you wish to call them) spend time together taking part in guided meditations, sharing any experiences, giving others healing, doing craft work, supporting one another, sitting in a circle together, doing rituals, meditating, doing divination and so on.

Depending on the ethos of the group, they can meet at full moon, the dark of the moon or the new moon – or a complete mix.

Bringing Lunar Energy inside

There are many ways in which you can bring lunar energy into your home. You can energise some water (preferably rain that you've collected) under a full moon and make essences with it, or use it for cleansing your home with a mixture of salt or essential oils. You can cleanse and charge crystals under the light of the moon and then place them around your home (Appendix 2).

I also have a variety of mirrors in my home, with round ones being used to represent full moon. You can hang small glitter balls, witch balls (commonly known today as friendship balls), mirrored wind chimes and crystals in your windows and fireplace and use them to repel any negative energies. With imagination, there are all kinds of ways to ensure lunar energy is in your home by the use of various representations.

A Moon Altar

You might decide you'd like an altar on which you keep your moon representations so they're readily available when you want to do your spell work. If you're fortunate enough to have a large outside space, you could choose a flat rock to display these. If not, a table inside is absolutely fine and probably most commonly used these days. Even a windowsill or bookshelf are fine to use.

As examples for your moon altar, you could place a black cloth with silver on it to represent the night and moon. Alternatively, you may choose a navy blue cloth and then place a round silver tray, bowl or mirror on it to represent the full moon. You could decorate the cloth with your chosen lunar goddess and her associations – colours, crystals and symbols. Or, if you're not working with a particular lunar goddess, you may simply choose to use a silver or white candle to represent her. So, decorate your altar with things you feel are feminine as the moon is feminine and also include any elemental representations you wish (Chapter 10). You will find a choice of altar cloths on the internet.

So get to know our lovely Lady Moon. Take a walk on a moonlit night and soak up her energy. Go into your garden and feel revitalised as you bathe in her lunar energy – then release it and send it back to the universe.

Traditional names for the full moon

Ancient cultures and tribes had various names for their full moons depending on the month in which they occurred. You can spend time choosing the names that appeal to you or mix and match them. All the names were related to activities that would be taking place during that month, themes or the weather. I think they're lovely – and I'm sure you can find many more, but these are just given so you can feel the importance of the moon in the times of our ancestors.

January – Old Moon, Wolf Moon, Winter Moon, Moon after Yule
February – Storm Moon, Ice Moon, Hunger Moon, Frost Moon
March – Crow Moon, Wind Moon, Plough Moon, Worm Moon
April – Awakening Moon, Pink Moon, Egg Moon, Seed Moon
May – Flower Moon, Milk Moon, Hare Moon, Bright Moon
June – Strawberry Moon, Mead Moon, Rose Moon
July – Thunder Moon, Herb Moon, Buck Moon, Summer Moon
August – Corn Moon, Grain Moon, Lightening Moon, Corn Moon
September – Barley Moon, Harvest Moon, Wine Moon
October – Hunter's Moon, Blood Moon, Blackberry Moon
November – Beaver Moon, Dark Moon, Mourning Moon
December – Cold Moon, Oak Moon, Long Night Moon

Planting by the moon

Planting by the moon is a practice that for those of us who have been brought up or lived in the country are fully aware of and many of us still plant by the moon today. If you watch any gardening/country programmes, reference is sometimes made by the presenters about the phase of the moon and what is ideal to plant under that phase.

As a guide – and if you're interested in researching this topic further – you can find out much more information on the internet, where you'll find lunar gardening tables to show the moon's cycles plus the astrological signs to help you choose the best planting dates. Briefly, here are some tips:

New moon – Plant annuals that produce their crops above the ground and their seed outside their fruit, such as broccoli, sprouts, cabbage, lettuce and cauliflower. Plant cereals and grains.

Waxing moon – Plant annuals whose seeds are inside the fruit, such as beans, peas, tomatoes, melons, peppers, cucumbers and pumpkins – plants that climb and may need staking.

Full moon to waning moon – Plant biennials, perennials, bulb and root plants, including parsnips, carrots, beetroots, potatoes, berries, trees and shrubs.

Isn't it fascinating how the lunar, solar and earth energies affect everything – and yet we pay such little attention to them?

Chapter 9 - Festivals of the Wheel of the Year (Earth Energy)

If you've read this far and are still interested in this wonderful spiritual journey, then let's take a walk on one of its other paths. You may well have heard about the Wheel of the Year, which is completely in tune with earth energy and is the final energy we'll be exploring. The Wheel of the Year is a name given in the mid 20th century to the ancient agricultural calendar which had been followed for centuries and celebrated the seasonal festivals.

Earth energy has an intimate connection with nature and the seasonal rhythms, with various festivals being celebrated through the year. As we work through each festival you'll learn the links to nature's cycles and if you can keep in flow with this energy as well, it'll bring rewards to your life. Earth energy, to me, is the slowest of the energies we live with – but there's always a festival ahead of us to celebrate.

Now seems to be the right time to mention the Goddess whose life is celebrated through these Wheel of the Year festivals. She's the substance of the universe, from whom everything comes into being. She's Mother Earth, the great mother, the great divine feminine. She's all around us - the earth, the moon, the planets, the stars, nature. She's the air we breathe. She's spirit or the Lady, whatever your special name may be for her. She sustains us on earth and provides us with everything we need – the food we eat, the water we drink, the medicinal remedies in plants that can be made into essential oils as well as traditional medicine and herbs for herbal remedies. She supplies it all. She also brings destruction that's necessary for life to continue and so is death as well as life. However, we can't control her – think of the earthquakes, tsunamis, volcanoes and other mass destruction that has taken place – but she can control us and it's this very point we need to respect. We belong to her, not her to us.

Our ancestors acknowledged their relationship with the earth and marked particular points in the year for celebrations. Over recent years these customs or folklores have been reclaimed and continue to be so. They have now become the eight festivals of the Wheel of the Year and are known as the sabbats.

Additionally, there are other celebrations (also known as rituals) that take place during the new and full moons. These are known as esbats, which simply means a celebration that isn't one of the eight main festivals/sabbats. At these esbats, rituals may be performed within a magic circle and may include healing for someone or sending out healing to Mother Earth. Esbats are also a time for celebratiion. Along with the esbats, there are also non-seasonal celebrations or rituals which are planned in when there's a need. These include naming, puberty rites, handfasting and crossing over ceremonies - plus of course initiation ceremonies if that's what you choose to do (see Appendix 6).

So for those of you who follow this path, you'll believe in an energy or life force that flows through us all and that everything and everyone is connected. We're nature lovers and environmentally conscious, living in tune with the natural world – trees, plants, rivers, oceans, the planets and stars. Everything's about balance and harmony – male and female, darkness and light, day and night, yin and yang – and it's this sense of balance and harmony that we constantly seek to achieve through living and working with the solar, lunar and earth energies as well as cleansing and looking after our own energy field.

So the Wheel of the Year isn't just about changing from one season to the next. Yes, it's obviously an acknowledgement of that but it's also about subtle changes in the earth's energy that affect us – just like the moon. So there's a need to follow that flow and direction of earth's energy and move with it.

We're now going to take a look at the eight seasonal festivals, the sabbats. For the purposes of this book, I'll be working through them as they occur in the northern hemisphere as I live in the UK. We'll start with Samhain (pronounced Sow-een) which is probably the most widely known festival with its links to Hallowe'en. The reason for starting with Samhain is because it's the "witches new year". As with our traditional new year, it's the beginning of the next cycle. The Wheel of the Year represents the life cycle from birth through life to death and re-birth and has lots of representations/associations within it which I'll be working through with you so you can incorporate them into your life and any celebrations you decide to have.

Samhain – This festival's celebrated on 31 October and is one of the four fire festivals in the Wheel of the Year. As already mentioned, it's the witches New Year's Eve. It's the ending of one year and the beginning of another as we celebrate the passing of the warmer autumn days and start embracing the darker, colder days ahead, moving into the months of darkness. Many cultures throughout the world celebrate a festival similar to Samhain and you may well have heard of the various Feasts of the Ancestors or Days of the Dead that take place, often continuing throughout November.

Traditionally it's the time to get prepared for the darkness and renewal ahead, plus being a time to honour our ancestors and the journeys they lived and sacrifices they made before us. A time for celebration, prayer and feasting as well as being the traditional time for divination work. On a mystical level, it's the time when the veil between the worlds is at its thinnest and spiritual beings are able to walk on the earth.

The crone aspect of the goddess is celebrated at Samhain. It's known as the season of the hag – or old woman. The crone goddess is the one who moves us from life to death. You may have heard of some of the crone goddesses - Rhiannon, the goddess of transition, Ceriddwen, the goddess of the cauldron of transformation or Hecate (sometimes spelt Hekate), the weaver of wisdom and guardian of the crossroads. The Samhain celebrations remind us that life contains death as well the mystery of re-birth or re-incarnation.

If you're wanting to observe tradition about honouring those who have gone before you, your celebrations might include placing a photo or an item that belonged to one of your loved ones who have passed on your altar, in your circle or somewhere in your home. You might decorate in the traditional colours of black and brown and spend time doing some meditation on the meaning of this festival. You could do some divination work and include the herbs rosemary (for remembrance) and thyme (for departed souls) in any rituals or spells. As part of your ritual, you could cut an apple (or pomegranate) in half and eat it as a symbolic gesture, leaving a cup of red wine or cake as an offering.

One of my Samhain altars

Yule – also known as The Winter Solstice or Midwinter. This festival takes place on 21 December and is about celebrating the rebirth of the sun. It's the time when the hours of darkness are at their maximum and light at its minimum and is the turning point because daylight hours slowly start to lengthen again.

Traditionally the Yule festival is about the birth of the sun and the battle between darkness and light – please don't think about darkness and light as good versus evil. The term evil does not exist on this spiritual path and is one mentioned in the Christian bible, hence their (d)evil. This spiritual path sees darkness and light complementing each other, forming a balance in our lives and providing for all our needs.

The battle between darkness and light is often represented as a fight between the Oak King (who represents light) and the Holly King (who represents darkness). The Oak King is triumphant at Yule. It's also the time of year when the goddess gives birth to the sun child, who in turn is the young sun god.

It's a time of inspiration and looking forward to the rest of the year – a time of beginnings, happiness and having fun. It's also a time for us to delve into deeper places and spend time in meditation.

So at this time of year, you might have a Yule log – traditionally made of oak - and you'd burn it as part of any ritual/ceremony you perform. You could keep some of the ash from it until the spring when you can sprinkle it on the soil as you plant out your seeds for the next harvest. It was believed to help with a good crop. Another tradition is to keep a small part of the Yule log and use it to start burning your Yule log the following year - again an indication to show how everything is linked and life is a circle/cycle.

To celebrate, light some candles to symbolise your desire to relight your inner sun. Meditate while doing this and let the candles burn down. Think about anything you want to do in the future and write your intentions on a piece of paper, keeping it safe and referring to it later in the year to see what you've achieved. You would usually be thinking about what you'd like to achieve in the coming six months, so up to the point of the Summer Solstice (being the time when you'd check what intentions you set at Yule).

If you wanted to be more traditional and really celebrate with family and friends, you could re-enact the battle of the Oak and Holly Kings. You could dress up in the traditional colours of Yule which are red, green and white and could make your own costumes and swords if you were feeling really advenutuous. Decorate your home with holly (for protection), ivy (for the promise that life lasts), mistletoe (for fertility) and other evergreens and have some on your altar. They remind us that earth will be green again.

One of my Yule altars

Imbolc – pronounced "im-olc". This festival celebrates the goddess' recovery from giving birth to the sun god at Yule and is another fire festival. The festival takes place on 1/2 February. Brighid (pronounced Breed) was the goddess in her maiden form and was a very popular goddess.

Her role is to breathe fire to awaken the earth again. She's a fire goddess and is associated with fertility, healing, blacksmithing, poetry and the hearth. It's a time to plant seeds and to think about things we wish to nurture and grow. It's a time of renewal and commitment to new projects. Winter is almost over - spring is on its way! Imbolc as a festival would have had a priestess presiding over the ceremony wearing a crown of lights. This is known as the white festival and is a time of cleansing, purification and new beginnings.

So how can you celebrate this festival? Some suggestions are to decorate your home and/or altar with fresh greenery and spring flowers. Snowdrops and primroses are traditional. Traditional colours for Imbolc are white, silver and gold so any other associations for your home/altar would be these colours.

If you decide on having a ritual, you could choose to drink milk as a toast to Brighid. As a Celtic goddess, this festival was celebrated at the time the sheep in Ireland were lactating, so milk became the traditional thing to drink. You could spend time making a Brighid's cross for your altar and a wand from an ash tree, the tree of Imbolc, placing both the cross and the wand in your fire when casting a spell. In ancient times the ash from the fire would have been sprinkled on to the land as fertiliser for the coming spring, similar to the Yule log tradition.

One of my Imbolc altars, including Brighid's cross

Another way to celebrate would be to make and wear a crown of lights. Using a garland and lighting candles is dangerous, so use a willow wreath with some battery operated lights wound through it. Or make a small crown from white clay and decorate it with white birthday candles. Make a wish as you light each candle and allow the candles to burn down naturally. This would not be for placing your head, but used as a representation of Brighid's crown. Make a wreath for your front door including white flowers, lights and ribbons.

My Imbolc wreath, displayed on my front door

Consider writing a poem about Imbolc and read it out during any ceremony or simply find a favourite poem and read that out. Anyway, just some ideas for you to consider.

Ostara – Also known as the Spring Equinox, Vernal Equinox or Eostre, taking place on 21 March. The hours of light and dark are equal again and the light is about to start gaining. The sun was a baby at Imbolc and is now a young man at the Spring Equinox.

The main symbols for this festival are the hare and the egg, which I'm sure are very familiar to you in relation to Easter. The hare (who has now become the Easter bunny) was believed to be a creature of the moon goddess who laid eggs at this time of year. The eggs represent potential life and fertility.

What can you do to celebrate this festival? You'll find some of the suggestions remarkably similar to the Easter activities we have.

Decorate some hard boiled eggs and have an egg hunt or decorate some hollow egg shells and hang them in your sacred place - may be on the branches of a tree where you sit and meditate. As eggs represent potential life, make a wish for something to come to fruition in the coming year.

Decorate your home and/or altar with daffodils and other spring flowers and anything in either red, yellow or gold which are the Ostara colours.

If you wanted to celebrate in a more traditional way, walk between a black and a white candle, pausing as you visualise yourself passing through a gateway into the summer months. Stop and think about what you need to balance more in your life as this is the festival when light and dark are equal/balanced.

One of my Ostara altars

Ostara is a gentle equinox compared to the others so get out into the fields and woods, looking for new shoots and buds - you may even want to plant something. See how it feels to hug a tree.

Beltane – This festival is the one most associated with fertility and is another fire festival. It's usually celebrated on 1 May, but celebrations can start on 30 April. Beltane means "bright fire" and it's the festival associated with the green man – a spirit/god of nature.

Traditionally, on May Day you had a maypole which represented the phallus. The ribbons on the maypole were considered to be female and as they are entwined up the pole, it represented a symbolic mating of the god and goddess. This in turn represented the time plants were beginning to grow and was a popular time for handfastings.

One of my Beltane altars

This is the one festival other faiths left alone and the maypole celebrations live on.

In the past, cattle would be driven between two fires to ensure their fertility before sending them out to pasture and our sexuality was celebrated with everyone staying up to see the sun rise.

In terms of celebrating, you could decorate your home, circle or altar with hawthorn, blackthorn or oak. Traditional colours are green, red and white. More recently, yellow and purple have been included. You could also light a bonfire. Nowadays you might use an incinerator of some sort or simply burn a candle. May Day celebrations still take place and a May Queen is elected.

Forfeit games are played and if you want to be very traditional, you could jump over a broomstick. Traditionally the handle represented the male and the brush, the female. As you do so, you might like to make promises to yourself or others present. Jumping over a broomstick is also a key part of any handfasting ceremony.

Litha – Also known as Midsummer or the Summer Solstice, Litha is celebrated on 21 June. It's a celebration of the longest day when the power of light is at its strongest, although this festival does have a hint of sadness because from now on the hours of darkness increase again.

The sun is now a middle aged man – a mighty warrior who has just reached his peak. There's another battle, traditionally represented as a fight between the Oak King (who represents light) and the Holly King (who represents darkness). The Holly King is triumphant this time.

Many stone circles were aligned with the rising midsummer sun. There are records over 700 years' old of bonfires being lit and torches being carried around the hillsides at this time of year.

In terms of celebrating, you would decorate your home with solar images, summer flowers – such as sunflowers and marigolds - and herbs. Litha's colours are gold and yellow.

It's the perfect time to be outside as much as possible, weather permitting, and having a picnic followed by a ritual. It's a time of drumming and telling each other stories and reciting poems as the sun sets. Go to the top of a hill and watch the sun go down.

You could make a crown or necklace from daisies or buttercups to wear during your celebrations.

Lammas – Also known as Lughnasadh (pronounced Loo-nah-sa), Lammas is traditionally celebrated on 1 August. It's the last of the four fire festivals and is celebrated as the first ear of wheat is cut. This is the time of year when the first crops are ripening – the early harvest. Its celebrations are based around having plenty.

Lammas means "loaf mass" from old English. There are many festivals world-wide that celebrate harvest, although it's believed the festival originated in Ireland as the name Lughnasadh comes from the Celtic sun god, Lugh.

Fruit is ripening and in a few weeks, we'll be descending into autumn. It's the time when the sun god is soon to end his reign, but it's a time of plenty and a time for living outdoors, festivals, sitting out in the garden until late. Even today the early August food fayres, festivals and markets that take place have their roots in these traditions.

We feel the pull to travel, to go walking, to visit friends just as the ancient tribes would have travelled many miles to meet up with other communities and celebrate the grain harvest. However, there's an awareness about this festival that it won't last forever.

This festival comes from the festival of Lugh, the Celtic sun god, and in the festival the sun god died in a ritual sacrifice. To remember Lugh, there were processions, feasts and athletic games in his honour. The festival is now seen as the beginning of the hunt for Lugh which culminates at Mabon, the next festival.

And so what about your celebrations? This is the time to harvest garden crops and be grateful, to pick our fruit, prepare and freeze them. Make jams and fruit pies for the darker months ahead. It's a time to feast on bread and cake with the first cutting of the grain. So, bake some bread and share it with your friends and family. Gather some herbs and make your own herbal teas – or make a smudge stick.

Make corn dollies - traditionally kept as a magical charm and good luck. You'll find plenty of tutorials on the internet. The corn dolly was originally made out of the last sheaf of corn to capture the "corn spirit". It was kept over the winter and was then returned to the fields in spring by either being burned or buried to ensure that the coming year's harvest would be successful. It's also time to start collecting seeds and storing them for later sowing. Play some team games to honour Lugh. Tribes would gather and show off their strength and endurance in competitive games.

Decorate your home with wheat, barley, oats, rye, sunflowers and marigolds – all things with solar symbolism. Make a cross from rowan tree twigs and hang it over your door for protection. Colours are pale yellow and orange for your altar cloth and any other representations in your home.

Mabon – Also known as the Autumn Equinox or Modron and it takes place on/around 23 September. This festival celebrates the culmination of the harvesting season and is a time when day and night are equal again.

It represents maturity – it's the time for rest after the season's hard work and also a time of rest within the Wheel of the Year as after the harvest has been gathered, we know we're in for a long, dark time ahead. Mabon marks the end of the hunt for Lugh who was believed to have hidden in the last sheaf of corn until it was cut down. His spirit, though, lives on in the seed grain. It's a time to give thanks for everything we've received through the year, both our food and our personal achievements. It's also time to make preparations to get through the days of darkness.

So decorate your home, circle or altar with harvest fruits, vegetables and autumn leaves. Colours are all shades of orange and rusts. Sit around a bonfire reflecting on everything you're grateful for. Make wine with the elderberries, blackberries, plums, apples and rosehips which are in abundance. Drink beer, mead or cider during any ritual or celebration. Slice an apple and as you eat it, reflect on the relevance of the five pointed star within it.

The Wheel of the Year festivals celebrate the solar journey through the year and its impact on earth. However, for me these festivals are far more connected with earth energy as we move through the seasons and celebrate how the land changes and what is produced to sustain us.

And then we return to Samhain, the festival at which we started - the completion of a circle as we've travelled through the Wheel of the Year - and so another new year begins as we continue our work with the earth's energy.

Chapter 10 - Working with the Elements

What are the elements? They're the building blocks of the entire universe, being the foundation of this spiritual path where nature is sacred and respected.

The elements of air, earth, fire, water and spirit are something you'll come across from time to time on your journey and regardless of how big or small a role they play in your personal spiritual path, they're something about which you should have some knowledge. Whether you want to incorporate them into your work is your decision, but for me they are fundamental components. We wouldn't exist without the elements – we wouldn't breathe without air, we'd die of thirst without water (as would every living animal and plant), we need the sun's energy for our health and to help our crops grow – and we need earth to provide us with everything in order to live our lives here.

When the elements are mentioned, the majority of people think of four - earth, air, fire and water. However, the other more elusive element is spirit. Spirit is the fifth element and is mystical and magical – it's something that can't be explained or described. When you're casting a spell, you may like to work with the symbolism and characteristics corresponding to each of the elemental energies, which are laid out in this chapter.

Please remember that correspondences can vary from tradition to tradition and also from person to person, although there are usually more similarities than differences. Although I consider myself to be eclectic and of no particular tradition, I never take any list of elemental correspondences as written and I change them to suit me - if something doesn't either feel right or work for me, then it's changed. You're free to do the same. You might also want to use the elemental symbols and carve them into a wand, broomstick or candle along with other symbols than mean something to you (such as planetary or astrological symbols).

Earth Element – The earth element is the one most closely linked with our physical world and is the densest energy of all the elements. It rules over money, property, business, security, health and responsibility. It's the foundation stone on which the other elements move. Its energy is receptive. It helps us to accept our responsibilities and limitations as well as being the grounding energy.

The earth element rules the astrological earth signs Taurus, Virgo and Capricorn. Earth personalities love to be surrounded by family. They're often quite tactile. They enjoy sensual pleasure. However, too much earth element slows down progress and too little brings a risk in the expansion of your projects/ideas. Below are some of the associations of the earth element.

The **symbol** for earth is:

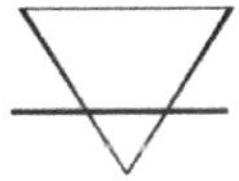

Gender: female
Energy: passive

Attributes:
Positive: ambitious, practical, responsible, steady, thorough, fertile, stable, productive, diligent
Negative: critical, inhibited, materialistic, possessive, slow, unforgiving, cold, solid, dull, stubborn

The earth element associations are:
Day of the week: Wednesday
Direction: north

Locations: caverns, the underworld, the womb, shelters, forests, fields
Sabbats: Samhain, Yule
Time of day: night
Time of life: death
Time of the year: winter
Colours: green, brown, black
Incense/Oils: patchouli, musk, vetiver
Plants/Herbs: barley, corn, oats, patchouli, potato, rhubarb, rye, vetiver, wheat, carrot, turnip – anything "earthy"
Minerals/Gems: green calcite, coal, salt, jasper, jet, malachite, peridot, black tourmaline, turquoise

<u>Air Element</u> – The air element governs the mind and all mental activity. As it's the element of the wind, air rules over all movement and is associated with travel, freedom, thought, ideas, intellect, imagination and discovery.

The air element governs the astrological air signs Gemini, Libra and Aquarius. Air personalities are rational, analytical, thinking clearly and don't rush into things. They enjoy mental stimulation, a good debate and an exchange of ideas. However, too little air makes for a critical outlook while too much can leave you living in a fantasy world and "away with the fairies".

The **symbol** for air is:

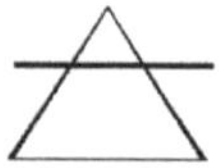

Gender: masculine
Energy: active

<u>Attributes:</u>
Positive: intelligent, communicative, inquisitive, inventive, literary, social, idealist, rational, technical

Negative: aloof, dispassionate, eccentric, unfocused, indecisive, deceptive, untrustworthy

The air element associations are:
Days of the week: Thursday, Saturday
Direction: east
Locations: mountain tops, sky, clouds
Sabbats: Imbolc, Ostara
Time of day: morning
Time of life: youth
Time of the year: spring
Colours: yellow, white, shades of grey and blue
Incense/Oils: sandalwood
Plants/Herbs: almond, borage, clover, dandelion, hazel, hops, marjoram, mint, parsley, pine, sage, lavender, mistletoe, bergamot, rice
Minerals/Gems: agates, jasper, pumice, aventurine, amethyst

Fire Element – The fire element is associated with the sun. Fire cleanses and purifies and is equally creative and destructive - it can destroy everything in its path but also has the power to transform anything it contacts. It's a fast, dynamic energy but as well as being inspirational, it can be frightening when it's out of control.

The fire element rules the astrological fire signs Aries, Leo and Sagittarius. Fire personalities are charming, charismatic and passionate. They live life to the full, relying on their instincts and intuition. Too much fire can be destructive because there are no boundaries and can result in selfishness and unrealistic expectations of other people. Too little fire results in low energy and a lack of motivation.

The **symbol** for fire is:

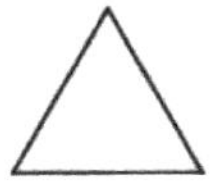

Gender: masculine
Energy: active

Attributes:
Positive: energetic, courageous, passionate, enthusiastic, intense, independent, optimistic, motivated
Negative: abrupt, excessive, domineering, impatient, hot headed, overbearing, selfish

The fire element associations are:
Days of the week: Sunday, Tuesday
Direction: south
Locations: deserts, volcanoes
Sabbats: Beltane, Litha
Time of day: midday
Time of life: young adulthood
Time of the year: summer
Colours: red, orange, gold
Incense/Oils: cinnamon, dragon's blood
Plants/Herbs: juniper, cinnamon, coriander, ginger, frankincense, holly, marigold, nutmeg, orange, rosemary, saffron, sunflower
Minerals/Gems: amber, obsidian, bloodstone, carnelian, citrine, tourmaline, quartz, sand, tiger's eye

The Water Element – The water element affects the subconscious, emotions and dreams – it's the element of love. Water's activity is always just beneath our surface, influencing our moods and emotional responses. It flows constantly.

The water element governs the astrological water signs Cancer, Scorpio and Pisces. Water personalities are spiritual, emotional, sensitive, empathetic and intuitive. They approach life from a feeling perspective rather than a thinking one. Too little water makes for emotional distance while too much water takes emotions to extremes and sometimes out of control.

The **symbol** for water is:

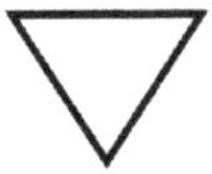

Gender: feminine
Energy: passive

Attributes:
Positive: compassionate, creative, receptive, intuitive, mysterious, resourceful, sensitive, cleansing, flexible
Negative: ambivalent, complex, deceptive, emotional, moody, over-sensitive, aggressive, selfish

The water element associations are:
Days of the week: Monday, Friday
Direction: west
Locations: seas, lakes, rivers, wells
Sabbats: Lughnasadh, Mabon
Time of day: twilight/sunset
Time of life: maturity
Time of the year: autumn
Colours: blue, silver, aquamarine
Incense/Oils: cypress, myrrh
Plants/Herbs: apple, sandalwood, blackberry, willow, chamomile, daisy, daffodil, vanilla, heather, jasmine, myrrh, rose, thyme
Minerals/Gems: blue lace agate, aquamarine, sapphire, sodalite, jade, pearl, lapis lazuli, moonstone

The Spirit Element – The fifth element is spirit and exists in the astral/spiritual realms. It's universal energy and is often expressed through art, music, writing, religion, magic, dancing, singing and healing – anything creative. It's divinity.

Spirit is usually associated with the crown chakra (and the outer body chakras, which are the spiritual chakras). Its colours are black and white, which are the colours containing or reflecting all light and darkness. It's also represented as violet as this colour is often used to represent psychic abilities and spirituality. Violet is also the colour associated with the crown chakra. If you use tarot cards, you'll generally find your High Priestess sitting between a black and a white pillar of some sort.

Spirit is everywhere and it unites everything. In our rituals it's our connection to the otherworlds/spiritual realms. It's present in all aspects of our lives and vibrates higher than human thoughts and emotions. It has no defined place or location like the other four elements, but we know it exists. Just as you know air is there, despite not being able to see it, because you're breathing.

It represents the life cycle - from birth through life to death and re-birth. No specific herbs or crystals correspond with it, but all of them do because everything is energetically connected. Whether we're aware of it or not, we're all part of this energy and energy connects us all.

As you can see, the elements are a rich, diverse and possibly a confusing, complex system of symbols and energies that affect our world and our spiritual practice. Working in harmony with them is a wonderful, spiritual experience so taking time to learn more about them is a very productive way to move forward from here. Take time to do some more research – you'll find elemental associations with animals, metals, birds, tarot cards, gods and goddesses – plus more. Learn about this fascinating subject so it becomes second nature to you.

The Pentagram – While we've been discovering elements, symbols and associations, it seems appropriate to mention the pentagram, the symbol most associated with this spiritual path. Each point of the pentagram represents one of the elements we've been learning about. This is why the pentagram, the five pointed star, is the ultimate symbol of balance – with equal points, all intertwined with each other—balance and harmony is key to our way of life. The pentagram is one single stroke when drawn, linking all the symbolic elements (points) together.

And so what is the circle around the pentagram? Well, it's there to represent the circle of life – of birth, life, death and rebirth and the energy that draws us all together as one. The circle pulls together all the elements as well as all creatures and everything derived from the elements – and it never ends. Within a circle, the symbol is knows as a pentacle.

The pentagram

The pentacle

Chapter 11 - The Altar and Its Tools

Now we're going to take a look at how you can put everything you've learnt so far into practice. The first thing you'll need to do is create your altar in your sacred place. This is a special place for you, where you can sit quietly and meditate. It might be in the corner of a room on a table, on a shelf, a windowsill or if you're fortunate enough, you might have a whole room you can decorate. Perhaps you've got an outside space that feels right to you for this work, or a summerhouse. The idea is that you can focus and connect with your higher self, goddess or spirit. You then place objects and images on your altar that mean something to you along with some traditional tools and anything that is relevant to the phase or astrological sign the moon is in. This might be the place where you keep your intentions through the lunar cycle – or until they come to fruition (and sometimes not). You might like to have a small jar or box on the altar in which to place them.

Certain objects are used for ritual purposes in all religions and this path is no exception. I believe tools amplify the energy of our rituals and symbolise those energies, particularly those of the elements, enhancing your link to the spiritual world.

They don't have any power in themselves except the power you give to them. It's usual if you're walking this path and have decided it's the one for you, you'd want your own craft tools. It isn't wise to touch someone else's tools without their permission, rather like you wouldn't touch their crystals or tarot cards. Even a quick touch may pass your personal energy to those tools, meaning lots of cleansing would need to be done afterwards.

You don't have to find perfect, expensive tools either – an item in a charity shop is fine if you're attracted to it – or you can make your own tools, which then seals them with your personal energy. Do remember that everything you buy will need cleansing.

The Altar

The basic purpose and design of any altar in any religion is to request the presence of who you believe in – for us, spirit/goddess. The word altar means "on high". Your altar can be made of anything and be inside or outside. It should always face the north (*the direction of power and manifestation*) and would have representations of the four elements, the goddess - and god if you wish - (even if just candles or pictures that resonate with you), a pentacle and basic ritual tools.

There are a few pictures of altars through this book which are ones I've decorated over the years for my own celebrations so will give you an idea of what can be done.

So here are some of the tools you can consider using on your altar:

A Wand

A wand has been used for thousands of years in magical practice. It evokes energy as well as directing and repelling it. It divides the earthly and spiritual worlds during circle casting and re-connects them when the circle is undone. It can also be used to draw magical symbols in the earthly or spiritual realms, as well as stirring around your brew in a cauldron – so it has lots of uses.

Your wand can simply be a stick of wood, often with the bark still on it. You can make your own and might want to research the properties of trees to decide which wood you want to use. If you choose to do this, set your intention as you go out into the woods looking for your wand - and always request permission before cutting any branches off a tree.

However, not all wands are made from wood. Some are made from copper tubes or glass. Some are made from metal or crystal and are decorated with gems or symbols carved along the handle with a gemstone on the tip, usually a clear quartz crystal. You can also use a crystal point or choose to make your own wand and personalise it with some of the symbols you've learnt about in this book - or using your own so it's your personal representation.

A Chalice

A chalice (sometimes known as a goblet) is used to represent feminine energy, fertility, the moon, emotions and the element of water. Its purpose is to gather and hold any energy. Having done this, it's believed to release it to the universe. It may be made of silver and engraved with a pentacle or another protection symbol but it can be made of any natural substance such as glass, clay, wood or other metal.

The chalice is used for the ceremonial drink or for offering a libation to the goddess. If you work in a group, it's often used to share appropriate drinks to mark celebrations at each of the sabbats: so if you recall the festivals of the year, you might drink milk at Imbolc, eggnog at Ostara, mead, beer or cider at Beltane, Litha, Lammas and Mabon and traditional red wine at Samhain and Yule. However, I sometimes just fill it with water and place on the altar to represent water in the west. So use it in whichever way is suitable to what you're doing.

An Athame

An athame (pronounced a-tha-may) is traditionally a black handled double-edged steel knife. Black absorbs power so any negative energy is absorbed and is transmuted and sent off to the universe.

The main purpose of the athame is to invoke and attract positive energy when you're doing your circle work. It can also be used to invoke the elements by drawing pentagrams at each quarter, but you may not feel ready for this quite yet.

<u>A Pentacle</u>
The main function of the pentacle is to protect but it also directs and grounds all the energies that are invited into your circle.

They're made from metals like copper, brass, silver or gold – or from wood, stone or resin and often decorated with symbols.

There are several types of pentacle and of course you can make your own. I've several in my home that I've made from twigs that I've bound together.

You may prefer a ritual pentacle for your altar – it's basically a flat disc with a pentagram in the middle of it and might have other symbols on it. You can also use it as the centrepiece of your altar.

<u>A Cauldron</u>
A cauldron was used for a variety of purposes in the past - for food, to make herbal remedies and medicines and to boil water. Every household had one, with it being in constant use throughout the day.

It symbolises the transformation that takes place during any rituals/spells, but also represents the womb of the goddess. It's a symbol of fertility, renewal and abundance.

Normally a cauldron is made of cast iron in order to hold the heat of anything burning within it, such as loose incense on a charcoal disc or any intentions. You can also use it to make black salt, for mixing herbs/potions and for scrying if you put water in it.

A Besom

A besom – or broomstick - is the oldest magical tool. It was used as an everyday household object and was often placed either near the hearth/fireplace or doors to protect unwanted visitors from entering. In fact this is still a bit of magic you can use today.

It's traditionally constructed of three woods: an ash handle (for protection), birch brush (for purification) and from willow for the binding (considered to be the goddess' sacred wood).

Besoms are most commonly used to cleanse the ritual area before casting a circle. The space is swept to represent negative energy being swept out of the area. They're also used to guard the opening into the circle.

At a handfasting a couple 'jump the broomstick' to cross the threshold of their new home ensuring fertility and domestic harmony as well as confirming their commitment to each other. During the Beltane festival, you might also jump the besom for purification, protection, fertility and abundance.

A Bell

Ringing a bell creates an energetic vibration which is powerful. In addition today we use cymbals, tuning forks and singing/crystal bowls, but for an altar and its work, I'd stick with the traditional bell.

It's a feminine symbol and can used for a variety of reasons within ritual. It's used to invoke the goddess, to banish negative energies, to prepare a sacred space, to mark different parts of a ritual, to signal a spell's beginning and ending or to mark the end of a group meditation.

A Boline

The boline is usually used for inscribing candles, carving runes and for chopping herbs/plants – in fact all the tasks other ritual tools can't do. It's smaller than the athame and traditionally has a white handle.

A Mortar and Pestle

These are traditionally a stone bowl (mortar) with a grinding implement (pestle) used to prepare herbs or other materials for healing or magic. However, there are many around made from other materials. The mortar represents the womb and the pestle, the phallus. They're used to crush or grind herbs, plants and resins and for making incenses for use in ritual work or for medicinal purposes. They help instil our personal energy into any work being done.

A Book of Shadows (BOS)

A BOS is a workbook or journal that contains rituals, prayers, invocations, spells, associations, personal experiences and practices along with any other information you want to include. I've included loads of articles in mine from magazines, books etc. In the past it would have been handwritten, but nowadays you'll find them typed up, photocopied or saved on a computer. It's the witch's book of rituals and magical information.

Information you find in someone else's BOS is only what they have learnt works for them, so don't ever feel you've got to believe or follow anyone else's words or rituals. It's up to you whether you allow others to read what you write in your BOS.

Candles

Candles are used today by all faiths to light altars as they're a symbol of bringing spiritual light into the darkness of the world. Bi-coloured candles, multi-coloured candles, floating candles and single coloured candles on the outside and another on the inside are all helpful when doing spells but all should be used in alignment with the intention of the spell. Use unscented candles (pure beeswax candles are the best, but more expensive) and inscribe symbols on them that are relevant to the work you're doing.

You can anoint them with an essential oil that corresponds to your magic/astrological sign to enhance your intention. The colour of the candle should also be aligned with your intention, although a white candle can be used for any intention.

Many of us feel we should never blow out a candle after spellwork. If you feel like this and it's not safe to leave the candle to burn down, use a candlesnuffer or clap your hands quickly over the flame but don't blow the candle out.

I often stand my candles in the sink – or place them outside - if I've decided they need to burn right down, but it all depends on what I'm doing. Candles are used to represent the goddess and god on your altar, simply to have some light while you're doing your ritual, to mark the elements, to represent fire or simply as a focal point for you.

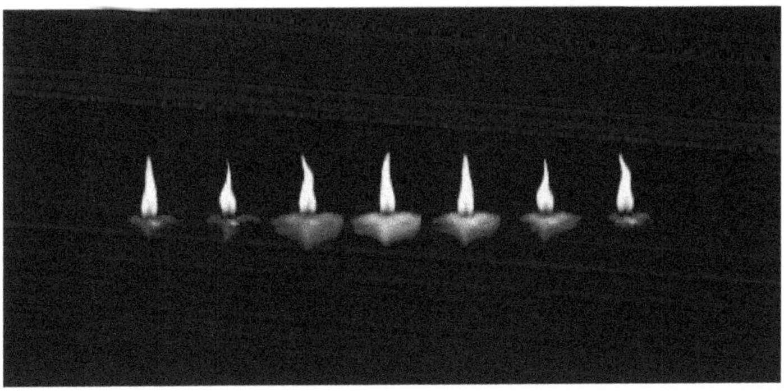

Chapter 12 - Cleansing Your Space and Aura

Creating a place where you can connect to the divine will help to enhance the spiritual work you're wanting to do, whether that's to celebrate any of the Wheel of the Year festivals, meditate, do some divination with your tarot cards or do some magic under the relevant phase/astrological sign of the moon. I believe having a sacred space is crucial. You might be fortunate enough to be able to dedicate a room in your home to this work, or have a shed/summerhouse you can use, a space in your garden or a table inside which is dedicated to your spiritual work and I promise it'll help you immensely. Just a space where you can go and connect.

When creating your space, you can refer to the various chapters in this book and choose what resonates with you to create, for instance, your altar. Or to choose any "tools" you want to buy to use in your work. It'll be in this space where all your spiritual work takes place and this will build up the energy of the area. You don't need loads of ornate objects, just things that appeal to you and mean something to you.

Before beginning any work in your sacred space, it's always important to cleanse the area. There are lots of ways to do this, but my favourite way is to use a bundle of sage or piece of palo santo wood. Using either of these will clear any negative energies in your space. You may also choose to use them both together if you feel the energy is quite dense. Equally you can buy both sage and palo santo as essential oils and can diffuse them in your space if you'd prefer not to burn.

Palo Santo wood and a sage bundle

You'll need a fireproof container to catch any ash if you do decide to burn, plus you may like to use a large feather to waft the smoke around the area you're cleansing. You can use this method to cleanse your crystals and other items for use in your spiritual work by passing them through the smoke. So, you'll light your bundle of sage or piece of palo santo wood and once it's smouldering, waft the smoke around your space to cleanse it, asking that any negative energies be gone. Do be aware the area can be left smelling a bit smoky for a couple of days and be conscious of any smoke alarms that could be set off if your sacred space is in your home.

Alternatively, if you're not overly keen on the idea of the smoke in your home, you could make up a spray which would include either sage or palo santo essential oil (or both) in water and spray it around the area you'll be working in. Another option is to burn some frankincense incense or make up a spray with frankincense essential oil, another good cleanser.

All these methods can be used to cleanse your aura as well. To do so, you'd pass a smouldering sage bundle or piece of palo santo wood around your body, ensuring the areas behind you, over your head and around your feet are also smudged (the term used for this work). You can also spray your aura in the same way with any sprays you've made up for cleansing purposes.

You might like to include some crystal chips that are known to dispel negative energy, such as black obsidian, in the sprays you make up. Before adding them, do leave them out under a full moon overnight to cleanse. I'd also leave them out in the sunlight for a few hours as this energetically charges the crystals and imbues them with both lunar and solar energy. If you're thinking of using any other crystals, do check they can be put in water.

Placing certain crystals around your sacred space helps absorb any negative energy, but I'd also use an additional method for cleansing.

Sound is another way to cleanse your space and your aura. Sound has its own purifying energy. There are crystal bowls, singing bowls, angel tuning forks and cymbals to name but a few which you "play" in your space/aura to cleanse the energy. A bell, wind chimes and even clapping are also used to break up any stagnant energy. Again, you might want to use an additional method of cleansing alongside the use of sound.

There are, of course, other ways in which you can cleanse your sacred space and aura but to me these more traditional methods are most effective. Once you practice cleansing your space and aura before any spiritual practice, I'm sure you'll feel a difference in the energy in which you're working.

Chapter 13 - Casting a Circle, Rituals & Spell Work

I want to make this as simple and straightforward as possible. Some circle casting and spell work is very ritualistic involving lots of chanting and energy raising. At this point you don't need to know about that and it's something you can look into as you go further on your spiritual journey. I like to keep things uncomplicated. You've probably already noticed in books you've read that before doing any rituals or spell work, you should cast a circle.

So, why do you need to do this and how? The purpose of casting a circle is to protect you and any others you're working with. It can also be useful to do the same before you start meditating if you're not using any other method of protecting yourself. You can simply visualise your circle as you cast it or you can define it with a ring of tea lights, stones, crystals or whatever appeals to you. Visualisation is certainly easier if you're working outside somewhere but you might like a more defined circle when you're working in your sacred space at home.

The circle's purpose is to protect your energy from any negative energies. I often visualise myself inside an igloo, cone or pyramid when I've cast my circle, knowing that I'm completely protected all around me – and beneath me - with whatever work I'm doing. Do be conscious that when you do this type of work, you're opening yourself up to the spiritual energetic realm and not all energies are positive. The circle also serves as protection for the energies you're working with.

As I said earlier, although there are lots of more advanced ritualistic ways of circle casting, rituals and spell work, my aim is to keep things simple and you can then advance from here once you're used to what you're doing and can make everything your own.

Casting a Circle

Be sure you won't be disturbed in your sacred place, whether that's at home, in your garden or if you've chosen to go out into nature. Do be aware of the directions – so know where your north, south, east and west are.

When first doing this, try using an exercise I was taught when I started exploring this path. You can record it and then play it back rather than trying to read these words.

Stand and face the east, the direction associated with mysticism, associated with air and the colour yellow. Close your eyes and think about what air means to you. Become conscious of the air you breathe and the wind in your hair. Ask the spirits of the east, the guardians of air, to help you learn and trust them.

Now turn to the south, associated with fire energy and the colour red. Close your eyes and think about what fire means to you - the warmth of the sun, orange sunsets on the horizon, blazing flames and simmering ashes. Ask the spirits of the south, the guardians of fire, to help you learn and trust them.

Now turn to the west, associated with water and emotions - and the colour blue. Close your eyes and think about what water means to you - the oceans, the rain, the water you drink that keeps you alive. Ask the spirits of the west, the guardians of water, to help you learn and trust them.

Turn and face the north, associated with earth and the colour green. Close your eyes and think about what earth means to you. Become conscious of the earth beneath your feet and its solid, stable energy. Ask the spirits of the north, the guardians of earth, to help you learn and trust them.

You may like to practice this the first few times you cast a circle and there'll be a different way of calling in the elements later in this chapter which you can do when you're more confident with what you're doing. This is an initial exercise to become attuned to the elements.

So, now you've acknowledged the elements and their directions, you can place a representation of every element at each point corresponding to east, south, west and north.

In the east you could light a stick of incense and place it in a holder, or place either a yellow feather, sage bundle or piece of palo santo wood. You could hang up some windchimes.

In the south you could place a small red pot of chilli (yes, be as inventive as you like), have an essential oil burner with a red tea light burning in it or just have a picture of a fire.

In the west, place a small bowl or cup of water. You might choose to place something there from the seaside, such as some seaweed or shells.

In the north, place a small dish in green or brown which has soil or salt in it. Put a small potted plant there, or a vase of flowers or some pebbles/a small rock or crystal.

Rather than placing these in the directions, you can also place them in the corresponding locations on your altar. In the centre of your circle, or the centre of your altar, place a white candle to represent spirit, the goddess, your higher consciousness – or whatever you like to refer to. You may also like to place a representation of their image in front of the candle.

Once you're confident with the initial exercise of recognising the presence of the elements and have a basic understanding of their energies, you can move to this more advanced way of opening your circle. You can also put in place all your elemental representations before calling in the elements and opening your circle.

East is the direction of the mystical and magical, which is why it's the starting point for opening your circle. You may like to move towards the easterly direction or stand in the centre of your circle and simply face the east, whichever feels right for you. Relax, breathe deeply until you feel calm, grounded and present. Then imagine the wind around you and become attuned to the element of air which should be helped by the initial exercise you'll have used several times. Simply stand and say "Spirits of the element of air, I ask you to join me in my circle."

Now turn to the south. Visualise crackling flames, the sun high in the sky and the embers of a fire. When you feel attuned to the element of fire, say "Spirits of the element of fire, I ask you to join me in my circle."

Turning to the west, imagine the waves of the ocean crashing into the seashore, the calmness of a brook with its water rippling by, standing under a waterfall and rain showers on your skin. When you feel attuned to the element of water say "Spirits of the element of water, I ask you to join me in my circle."

Now turn to the north and become aware of the smell of grass after it's rained, see yourself sitting in a cave, deep in the earth and hear the silence, try and feel your bare feet on the soil. When you feel attuned to the element of earth say "Spirits of the element of earth, I ask you to join me in my circle."

Now either in the centre of your circle if that's where you've placed your white candle, or standing in front of your altar (which should always be in the northerly direction) if that's where you've placed your candle, become aware of your feet. Send a column of light – or some roots if that's easier to visualise – into the centre of the earth. See a golden light, earth's grounding energy, travelling back up into you and your aura. Then see a ball of dazzling white light above your head and draw down the white energy into your body and aura through your crown chakra. When you feel you're grounded and protected for your work in your circle, say "Spirit/goddess I ask you to join me in my circle."

If it feels right to you, you might want to raise your arms whilst calling in the elements. Feel protected and grounded, knowing you can safely do your ritual and/or spell work now you've cast your circle. So, now it's time to do whatever work you're wanting to do ensuring you stay inside your circle, your space of protection, to do your spiritual activities.

For now, remember to always open your circle moving in a clockwise direction. There are times when you would move anti-clockwise, but it's not for this book. As you become more advanced, if you have a besom (broomstick), you can walk around the circle in a clockwise direction brushing away any negativity from your space and cast your circle in the traditional way before you start placing your representations in the directions. Just make sure the besom doesn't touch the floor.

Rituals

Put simply, a ritual is a ceremony which consists of performing a series of actions in a set order/sequence. These always occur within the protection of a circle. There are many rituals that you can do, but in the main these are performed when celebrating the festivals of the Wheel of the Year as well as full and new moon rituals. In addition, there are other rituals such as initiation, handfasting, naming and crossing over. So, you might want to use a ritual to celebrate the festivals, briefly described below:

Samhain: the end of summer and beginning of winter; the night the veils are thin and we can communicate with out ancestors
Yule: celebrates the goddess giving birth to the sun god
Imbolc: the first signs of spring, as well as a time of spiritual cleansing and re-dedication to the goddess
Ostara: celebrates longer days and shorter nights and the union of the god and goddess, symbolising fertility
Beltane: the end of the planting season and sexuality
Litha: the peak of the sun god's power, involving the lighting of bonfires
Lammas: the early harvest, a time when the goddess surrenders control to the god. A time to feast!
Mabon: the balance between light and dark and the late harvest

Firstly decide why you want to conduct a ritual and ensure your intention is clear. Decide how you want to perform your ritual, writing down any words you want to use or chant during the ritual.

You'll have placed all the tools and necessary objects relevant to your intention/ritual in your circle already.

You may like to invoke (call in) a particular deity that you associate with the ritual you're about to perform. You'll then conduct your ritual in any way that feels right to you. You could include some meditation with a particular crystal, share some food with others (particularly at the harvest festivals) and include some craftwork that represents what you want to achieve.

You'll find many rituals on line but writing your own will always be more powerful. So initially look at others' rituals and take away from them what resonates with you, but as you practice, you'll soon be able to do your own simply by reference to the information in this book.

However, you don't have to perform a ritual each time you decide to cast a circle. You might simply want a circle to protect you for meditation or for some other reason such as spell work.

Spell work

Spell work is also associated with rituals. However, although you can do a spell as part of your ritual, you may simply want to cast a circle in order to protect yourself while doing your spell. You don't always have to include a ritual. Spell work is done to make a positive change in your life. It may include a spell for love, for healing or for prosperity. Again, there are many, many books as well as spells on line that you can use until you feel confident in your own spell creating. Remember to incorporate all the associations I've spoken about earlier in this book to add your own touch of magic.

Closing the Circle

So your work is done and now you're wanting to finish and close down your circle. You need to thank each of the elements and spirit/the goddess for their presence with you.

You'll need to stand again and starting at the centre of your circle or in front of you altar, focus on spirit/the goddess and say "Spirit/goddess thank you for being with me in my circle".

To close down a circle, you walk in an anti-clockwise direction. Face the north reflecting on the element of earth (or move to the northerly direction) and say "Earth, thank you for being with me in my circle".

Then move to the westerly direction – or just turn to face the west - think of the element of water and say "Water, thank you for being with me in my circle".

Move to face the south – or move to the south - think of the element of fire and say "Fire, thank you for being with me in my circle".

Move to face the east - or move to the east - thinking of the element of air and say "Air, thank you for being with me in my circle".

Then say the words "Blessed be. So mote it be". Your circle is now closed and you can visualise the energy that you've raised within it blowing away into the universe, believing it'll do its work.

This may seem a lot to practice and remember, but it'll become second nature to you if you keep practicing. As time goes by, you'll learn to change and enhance the words you use but to start with, this is enough.

And that is it. You've now cast your circle, done a ritual and some spellwork and closed down your circle. I do hope you've enjoyed your journey through my book. I believe if you put what you've learnt into practice and live in tune with the universe, you'll have a wonderful lifelong experience of the spiritual realms.

Appendix 1 - A bit about Terminology

Oh and doesn't terminology get complicated! So many words meaning virtually the same thing. I've struggled to understand the meaning of some words that I've seen used, so I've tried to group them, or give a simple explanation. I've included below some of the ones I've used to try to simplify any confusion there may be.

Associations are representations/correspondences.

Astrological signs are the same as the sun signs, zodiac signs, star signs or birth signs.

Blessed Be literally means "be blessed" and when said means that person is willing good things to happen to them or to others.

Divination means seeking to know the unknown by supernatural means. This would include palm reading, reading tarot cards, runes or using a crystal ball, to name a few. Seeking to know the future.

Esoteric literally means secret, with the implication that this path is only understood and/or appreciated by a small group of people who are enlightened. Hence it's often linked to magical practice.

Intention means making a wish, planning for a specific outcome, dreaming of what you're wanting to happen or making magic.

A libation is a liquid offering to a deity.

Manifesting is the same as coming to fruition or completion – it's the outcome.

Solitary means practising alone and not as part of a coven.

So Mote it Be means "so must it be" or "so it will be" or "and so it is" and is traditionally said at the end of a ritual or spell work.

A talisman is an amulet - a good luck charm.

Universe, spirit, universal life force, goddess, god, higher consciousness, the management, "them upstairs", your higher self, your higher consciousness, the Lady all mean the same. It's whoever you believe in and want to call "it".

Appendix 2 - Cleansing and Charging of Your Crystals

Some of this information is already mentioned in Chapter 12, but for clarity, I'll repeat some of it here.

There are various ways you can cleanse your crystals and I can understand why people become confused with so many options that you can find on the internet. My approach is quite traditional and I prefer to work with the tried and tested ways, even though they might take longer. Again, it's all down to what resonates with you but there are a lot of short cuts out there, which I wouldn't advise adopting.

My preferred way is to leave out the crystals you're wanting to work with overnight under the full moon. In addition, I then leave them out in the daylight for a few hours, but you need to be careful with the sun because it can fade the crystals. To me, this energetically charges the crystals and gives them balance - both lunar and solar energy. In addition the majority of crystals can be placed in water but do be careful as some can't – for instance, selenite, malachite, calcite and kyanite – so please check. You can place "waterproof" crystals out under the moon in a bowl of spring water. You can then use the lunar charged water to make various sprays for spiritual work. Obviously dry your crystals once cleansed.

Another option is to leave them out under the full moon in salt water (salt is a traditional cleansing method) but again you'd need to check the crystal is both water and salt tolerant. The next morning you'd rinse the crystals to remove the salt and dry them – and you could also use the salt water for any other cleansing you might be doing in your spiritual work or simply dispose of it. You can also leave them out in daylight as previously mentioned.

Other options are:

a) Dry salt – if you're sure the crystals are salt tolerant, you can leave them in a glass bowl filled with salt and bury the crystals, leaving them overnight. The salt will need to be thrown away as it's believed to hold negative energy once used and doesn't disperse it.

b) Leave your crystals on a large piece of selenite or amethyst for 24-48 hours. Or if you have a crystal bowl made of either of these crystals, you can place them in it. I've got a selenite bowl that I sometimes use and both crystals are known to cleanse other crystals.

c) There are various things you can use to "smoke" the crystals and cleanse them by passing the crystal through the smoke. So you might choose sandalwood or frankincense incense, a sage bundle or palo santo wood (which is my personal favourite). The smoke purifies the crystals.

d) Sound is another way to cleanse. There are crystal bowls, singing bowls, angel tuning forks, a bell, cymbals and windchimes which you can play around the crystals to cleanse the energy. Clapping is also used to break up any negative energy.

e) Brown rice is believed to absorb all negativity, so you put your crystals in a bowl of it overnight and then remove them the following day. The brown rice will need to be thrown away as it's believed to hold negative energy once used and doesn't disperse it.

f) You can channel or visualise divine white light into the crystals.

g) If you are Reiki 2 trained, you can cleanse your crystals by using the Reiki power symbol.

These are just some ways to cleanse your crystals. I use a couple of these alternatives when I need to cleanse a crystal and there's not a full moon, so it's useful to be aware of different ways you can cleanse. However, for me the full moon is by far the best and most effective way.

Once your crystals are cleansed they'll need to be programmed or energised for use. This is about intention setting. I do a few minutes meditation holding the crystal I'm wanting to use in my hand and focussing on what I'm wanting to use it for. This energetically connects you to the crystal and sets out its purpose. Another way is to lie back and place the crystal on your third eye and do the same. You're basically communicating with the crystal and asking for its help with whatever you're seeking to do/achieve - and always remember to say thank you.

Appendix 3 - Making a Talisman

A talisman – or an amulet - is an object that you believe holds magical properties, providing a particular power, energy and/or protection for you. It's also known as a good luck charm. It's normally fairly small in size and used for specific purposes. If you decide to make one, you'll find all the associations in this book a useful starting point.

A talisman can be made from anything – gems, stones, plants, herbs, metal, wood – and making one might be an activity when you're in your circle. The owner of the talisman carries it with them or keeps it in a special place they might be wanting to influence – eg in your purse if you're wanting to attract more money. Or if you carry one, you can touch it to remind you of something important or can use it in stressful situations to keep you calm.

Having a talisman can also help protect you from negative energies – I'm sure we all know people who seem to completely drain us when we're in their company, so you could use some protection crystals in your talisman to absorb the negative energy and protect your own energy.

However, it's for you to "charge" your talisman for whatever you want it to help you with - so to attract more love into your life, more money, general good luck, good health, to name a few. Here's my simple way to make a talisman once you've cast your circle:

(a) Choose something that represents what you're wanting to use your talisman for, so perhaps a small coin for attracting money, a ring or some rose petals if you're wanting to attract love...anything that means something to you. A small picture will do – it's all about intention.

(b) Spend a few minutes in your circle holding the object you've chosen while you meditate. Ask whoever you believe in that their energy fills and surrounds your chosen object. This is very similar to intention setting, with your object being the physical representation of what you're wishing for – good luck, protection etc. This is what is called "charging" your talisman, just as you would charge crystals.

(c) Now place your charged object in a small material pouch which has drawstrings. You could even make your own pouch so the talisman is completely surrounded with your energy. This means anything else you add, such as herbs, is kept together in one place. Don't allow anyone else to touch it.

(d) Now put any other associations in the pouch with your charged object to enhance your intention. You might add a symbol, such as a pentagram, some petals, a crystal, a leaf from a particular plant or put some essential oil on the pouch – just whatever seems right to you.

(e) You then need to "seal" the talisman pouch symbolically. For this, draw a symbol over it – perhaps an astrological or elemental symbol you associate with your talisman. So if you've done your working under the Leo moon, you may decide to use the symbol of Leo. Leo is a fire sign, so you might choose to seal it with the elemental sign for fire – or even use both.

(f) Sleep with your talisman under your pillow overnight and the next morning place your talisman where you want it to be and let it do its work.

Remember that like crystals, a talisman will need to be re-charged from time to time, so if you sense your talisman's effectiveness is reducing, repeat (b) above. Having a talisman about can help you feel better, more confident and secure.

Appendix 4 - Crystal Essences and Elixirs

Crystals – or gems – essences and elixirs – are known by many names: crystal water, elixir water, gem water, healing elixirs or tonics, crystal tonics, gem tonics and they've been used throughout the ages. They're an easy way to use the energies of crystals for healing, magic, sprays etc and are easy to make. To make things easy, I'll just refer to "crystal essences" as making these is basically infusing water with the crystal's/crystals' energy and isn't complicated. However simple this may seem, I love to think of these essences as mystical and magical.

I also believe the healing properties of crystals are very strong when they're infused in your drinking water and if you don't know very much about crystals and their energy, this might be the easiest way to find out. It's probably the simplest of crystal essences. You can use essences by drinking them, adding them to your bath water, rubbing them into your wrists, rubbing them on to your chakras, spraying your aura to cleanse it or simply by rubbing the water into the palms of your hands and just breathing it in. Again, it's all about your intention and what you're wanting to use your crystal(s) for.

So you can make crystal essences for immediate use, which can be stored in a sealed container in the fridge for a few days, or you can make them for longer term use by adding some vodka, which is a preservative. If you do Reiki, you can charge the water with the Reiki power symbol. By making your own essences, you can experiment with different types of crystals to find out what really works for you.

So to start with, I'm suggesting some crystals you can work with before going into more depth about the energy of crystals. There are so many crystals that it's sometimes difficult to keep up.

Clear Quartz – known as an overall healer or the master healer, its energy is about cleansing, being focused, clarity, being positive and present.

Rose Quartz – a pale pink crystal used to help with emotional issues. It's all about compassion, forgiveness, love and enabling communication about emotions with others. It's also the crystal to work with for self-love which we often find hard.

Amethyst – a crystal that is found in shades of pale lavender through to violet and is used to help you feel calm and relaxed. It helps with mental health issues, intuition, dreams and creativity. Its energy is very peaceful.

Smoky Quartz – helps you "get your feet on the ground". It helps you relax and centre, plus being a good protective crystal. It is found in varying shades of brown.

Black Obsidian – a crystal that helps give you courage to achieve. It releases negative energy and is protective – it's one I use a lot.

Just a word of warning before you think about using other crystals, you need to be aware which crystals can't be placed in water. These are known as "soft" crystals and will end up dissolving. As a general guide, with a few exceptions, stones that end in "ite" tend to dissolve in water and are not safe for drinking water – kyanite and selenite, for example. I had a beautiful selenite palm stone and – unaware of the damage water could do – placed it in a bowl of water overnight under the full moon. I was so disappointed to find my beautiful palm stone looking dull after I dried it off the next morning. Its lovely sheen had completely disappeared. So if you're wanting to use one of these crystals, you can tape them to the side of the water container you're using. Alternatively you can put your water container into a bowl and place the crystal or crystals in the bowl.

In addition, you need to be aware that some crystals aren't safe when added to drinking water. This is because a few of them can corrode and some contain minerals or radiation that make them unfit for human consumption. So you really must check out the properties of the crystals you're wanting to work with and may decide the safest way is to either tape the crystal to the side of the water container or pop it in a bowl which holds your water container.

Preparations for a crystal essence

Choose the crystal(s) whose energy you want in your essence. Cleanse them under the full moon – or by one of the other methods I've suggested in Appendix 2 and "charge" them for use. You'll also want some lunar charged water. You can either use some you've charged under the full moon previously, or you can put your completed crystal essence out under the full moon to charge the water.

You'll also need a spray bottle (brown, green or blue glass is preferable) and a bowl/bowls in which to put your water container(s) if you're using crystals that don't mix well in water. If you've not already got any lunar charged water, you'll need some spring or distilled water, although rain water is my preferred choice. If you're wanting to preserve your essence for longer term use, then you'll also need some vodka. Do this work in a circle of protection and you might want to check the moon phase and astrological sign of the moon to enhance your work.

So now you're in your circle with all your "ingredients". Ground and protect yourself and you might want to meditate holding the crystal(s) you're going to be using in your essence. Meditating with the crystal(s) you're creating your essence with will be more powerful. Set your intention and visualise your crystal(s) being infused with power. You can state your intention for the essence out loud, which also adds power to your work – and ask that its use is for the highest good.

Place the crystal(s) in your spray bottle. Carefully pour water into it/them – you might want to use a small funnel or pipette for this. Seal it tightly.

If you're using a crystal that dissolves, simply pour the water into your spray bottle and seal it. Place it into your bowl. Then arrange the crystal(s) around the outside of the container pointing it/them towards the spray bottle. Again state your intention aloud and ask for spiritual intervention to imbue your crystal with energy to be used for the highest good. If your water hasn't already been lunar charged, leave the spray bottle and bowl under the moonlight overnight. You can now use this essence for a few days.

However, If you're wanting a longer term essence, you'll need to pour out half the lunar charged water into another container, which can then be used to make an additional spray. Then fill the remainder of the bottle with vodka, which will preserve it. Seal it and store it safely for future use. If you'd like to, you can add a drop or two of essential oil(s) to the essence.

Appendix 5 - A Little Something About Meditation

I really believe meditation to be an important aspect of this way of life and feel it's key to our spiritual practice. However, I'm also aware that others feel meditation is not for this spiritual path and is more akin to Buddhism – it can become a polarising topic so I'm only talking about my opinion and it's for you to decide whether or not you'll use it.

To me, meditation can become a great way to prepare to harness the power of your mind during your spell work and it also trains us to quieten our mind and stop listening to all that mental "chatter" that goes on. When that's under control, we can connect more deeply to our spirituality and listen more clearly to our intuition. However, I completely get you if you say you can't reduce the chatter, you find it boring, can't relate to it and don't see any benefit from it. I used to feel that way - my journey with meditation can only be described as rocky, but over the years I continued to practice until I reached the place where I now am.

Well before the practice of meditation, spells were cast using crystals, oils, herbs, candles, lunar energy and they still worked. Magic comes from within ourselves. We have powerful minds and when they're focused, they produce results. So before meditation, magic still happened. However visualisation meditations can reinforce your intentions by taking you through all the detail of how to reach the outcome you're seeking. You can pre-record these visualistations and then meditate with them.

There are loads of different types of meditation – movement meditation, mindfulness, mantra meditation, transcendental meditation, guided meditation and the one that I love, visualisation.

Overall, the main aim of meditation is about training your mind. It can be used for reducing stress and depression, inducing relaxation and a feeling of calm as well as improving your general wellbeing. You have to decide whether any of these apply to your spiritual journey.

My decision is they do, as being in a better mind set when doing or preparing for any spiritual work can only be of benefit - only my opinion.

Do take time to practice meditation. Try putting on some calming music and ask to connect with the spiritual realms. Become aware of your own energy. Cleanse your aura and chakras from any negativity by listening to a chakra cleansing visualisation meditation. You'll eventually find yourself entering a trance like state which is basically a new level of energetic awareness and helps you with your spiritual work, taking you on journeys to the other worlds. Meditation can also be used for your own personal healing - healing from traumas of the past and even from past lives.

However, if meditation doesn't feel right for you or the results don't feel good, try going for a walk or run in the country, try dancing, singing, chanting, drawing or painting to raise your vibration - whatever works for you is right for you.

Appendix 6 - Our traditional Rituals

I thought it might be helpful to give you a bit more information about some additional rituals – or ceremonies - celebrated on this path. You've already explored the Wheel of the Year and ideas for rituals that might take place then, so this adds to the knowledge you already have. These old ceremonies are being practiced increasingly again today and becoming more popular.

Naming Ceremony

This ceremony is for a baby or child when they are officially given their name. Parents choose their child's guardians, rather like godparents, who take part in the ceremony. Other members of the family and friends also take part. These are all symbolic gestures and have no legal bearing. Parents are involved in arranging the ceremony with whoever resides over it. The baby/child is blessed at the ceremony.

Puberty Rites/Coming of Age Ceremony

This is a celebration of the passage of a young person into maturity and is a mark of respect to acknowledge this time in their lives. The age thirteen is often recognised as the number of transition so celebrations take place around the young person's 13th birthday, but this is flexible. It might be the young person wants to dedicate themselves to the beliefs of this spiritual path and can be welcomed into it. Celebrations also take place when a young woman starts her periods to acknowledge her transition to womanhood. This is a lovely way to remove any fear or shame from the onset of puberty/adolescence.

Handfasting Ceremony

Handfasting is an ancient symbolic ritual where a couple stand face to face while their hands are tied together with ribbons of their choice, hence the saying "tying the knot".

Traditionally the commitment was for a year and a day and then the couple could either re-commit or part company. As their hands were tied, they say words they have generally written themselves to express their commitment to each other. This is the ceremony which involves jumping over the broomstick. They keep the ribbons that bound their hands as a momento of the vows they make.

Passing Over Ceremony

This ceremony is to say goodbye to someone. It is believed the ceremony helps the person's spirit pass over to the next phase of their spiritual journey. The ceremony focuses on them, their life and the new adventure they'll be beginning. This path believes we pass to the Summerland and today the ceremony may include a guided meditation to the edge of the Summerland. Poetry may be read out, with those present contributing to the ceremony in some way.

Initiation Ceremony

If you're completely committed to following this path, you may decide to dedicate yourself to following it as a way of life. At this point you may have thought about having an initiation ceremony. You can do this by yourself or can be initiated in a group setting, which can be either formal or informal. If it's a very traditional initiation, there's likely to be quite a lot of secrecy about the ceremony and it's not something to be taken likely. However, you can also do an individual, or solitary, dedication yourself which would be on your terms and is strictly between you and the goddess.

Full Moon Ritual

A full moon ritual is a series of symbolic actions taken on the night of the full moon to tap into the potential of the full moon energy. It's a time to celebrate and represents things coming to fruition, a time of completion, bringing a lot of energy with it. It's also the time of forgiving, being grateful, releasing and healing as you move forward into the waning moon phase of the lunar cycle.

If you can, do your ritual outside and allow the moonlight to shine on you. Dance to some music to shift any stagnant energy from your body and around your aura; chant if you want to. You can write your own rituals, using your knowledge about the astrological sign the moon is in and all its associations.

Dark or New Moon Ritual

The dark or new moon breathes fresh energy into any area of your life where you'd like to see some change ahead. It's the time of intention setting, of sowing a seed. It's the beginning of a new lunar cycle and the perfect time to plan to manifest something new that you want to create and experience in your life. You can write your own rituals based on what you want to commit to doing. They can be very simple, such as looking after yourself more, meditating more regularly or taking up yoga – or you can make them as complicated as you like. Again use your knowledge about the astrological sign the new moon is in at the time to write your ritual.

I hope you've found these brief explanations of use to you and you'll explore them far more as you continue your spiritual journey. If you'd like to know more, please contact me at mooncrafting@outlook.com or pop across to my website at www.mooncrafting.com.

Lightning Source UK Ltd.
Milton Keynes UK
UKHW010702301222
414627UK00001B/188